BLESSED IS SHE WHO Believed

Theresa Ann Reyna

Starfish Press
LLC

Blessed is She Who Believed: Faith for the Miraculous
Copyright © 2022 Theresa Ann Reyna

All rights reserved. No part of this book may be used or reproduced by any means, graphic, electronic, or mechanical, including photocopying, recording, taping or by any information storage retrieval system without the written permission of the publisher except in the case of brief quotations embodied in critical articles and reviews.

This book is a work of non-fiction. Unless otherwise noted, the author and the publisher make no explicit guarantees as to the accuracy of the information contained in this book and in some cases, names of people and places have been altered to protect their privacy.

Starfish Press, LLC books may be ordered through booksellers or by contacting:

Starfish Press, LLC
59 Northrup Drive
Franklin, NC 28734
www.starfish-press.com

Edited by: Jessica Hallmark
Book Design by: Jessica Hallmark
Cover Design by: Jessica Hallmark
www.jessicahallmark.com

ISBN: 978-1-953129-09-3 (Paperback)
ISBN: 978-1-953129-10-9 (Hardcover)
ISBN: 978-1-953129-11-6 (EPUB)

Library of Congress Control Number: 2022950951

Scripture quotations marked NKJV are taken from the New King James Version®. Copyright © 1982 by Thomas Nelson. Used by permission. All rights reserved.

Scripture quotations marked NASB® are taken from the New American Standard Bible®, Copyright © 1960, 1971, 1977, 1995, 2020 by The Lockman Foundation. Used by permission. All rights reserved. www.Lockman.org.

Scripture quotations marked TPT are from The Passion Translation®. Copyright © 2017, 2018, 2020 by Passion & Fire Ministries, Inc. Used by permission. All rights reserved. www.ThePassionTranslation.com.

Scripture quotations marked (NLT) are taken from the Holy Bible, New Living Translation, copyright ©1996, 2004, 2015 by Tyndale House Foundation. Used by permission of Tyndale House Publishers, Carol Stream, Illinois 60188. All rights reserved.

Scripture quotations marked AMP are taken from the Amplified® Bible, Copyright © 2015 by The Lockman Foundation. Used by permission. www.Lockman.org.

Scripture quotations marked (TLB) are taken from The Living Bible copyright © 1971. Used by permission of Tyndale House Publishers, Carol Stream, Illinois 60188. All rights reserved.

Scripture quotations marked (ESV) are from The ESV® Bible (The Holy Bible, English Standard Version®), copyright © 2001 by Crossway, a publishing ministry of Good News Publishers. Used by permission. All rights reserved.

Scripture quotations marked NIV are taken from The Holy Bible, New International Version® NIV® Copyright © 1973 1978 1984 2011 by Biblica, Inc.™ Used by permission. All rights reserved worldwide.

Scripture quotations marked CSB have been taken from the Christian Standard Bible®, Copyright © 2017 by Holman Bible Publishers. Used by permission. Christian Standard Bible® and CSB® are federally registered trademarks of Holman Bible Publishers.

Scripture quotations marked JUB are taken from the Jubilee Bible, copyright © 2000, 2001, 2010, 2013 by Life Sentence Publishing, Inc. Used by permission of Life Sentence Publishing, Inc., Abbotsford, Wisconsin. All rights reserved.

Scripture quotations marked KJV are taken from the King James Version of the Bible.

Scripture quotations marked ASV are taken from the American Standard Version of the Bible.

Scripture quotations marked GW is taken from GOD'S WORD®. © 1995, 2003, 2013, 2014, 2019, 2020 by God's Word to the Nations Mission Society. Used by permission.

Contents

Dedication..ix
Introduction..xi

Chapter 1   Mary: God's Woman of Faith...1
            Overshadowed by the Holy Spirit – The Seed of Christ...........10
            It's Time to Birth!..16

Chapter 2   A Living Sacrifice: Holy and Acceptable........................23
            A Sword Will Enter Your Heart......................................28
            The Fellowship of Suffering..31
            Who is My Brother, Sister, and Mother?............................38

Chapter 3   The Divine Turnaround..43
            Discerning the Time...54
            The Great Divide..62
            God's 11th Hour Workers..71

Chapter 4   The Upper Room of Power...88
            The Release of the Holy Spirit's Power.............................97
            The Spirit of Unity...108
            Walking in Miracle Power...118

Chapter 5	The Spirit and the Bride say: "Come!"......................127
	The Fullness of Time – No More Delay!........................133
	God's End-Time Revelations through Dreams and Visions......149
	The Bride has Made Herself Ready...............................161
	The Wedding Feast of Cana – The Third Day..............173

Conclusion..185
Bibliography..189
Acknowledgments..193
About the Author..194

DEDICATION

With all my heart I dedicate this book to every child of God who has believed that the Lord would fulfill His promises to them and are walking in the "High Place" with Him. I also dedicate this book to everyone who is in a "dark valley" but are still standing strong in faith and believing every promise that Jesus has spoken to them. Keep pressing in, for God will not fail to complete His glorious work in and through your life in this hour.

To:

My loving children and grandchildren: You are a special treasure to me, and I continue to stand on every promise that the Lord has given me concerning the glorious future that He has planned for your lives. You are loved; you are blessed, and I know in this glorious *new day* you will receive all that God has for your lives.

Ron, I love you; thanks for giving me "space" to work on this book. Thanks for *pulling me away* from my work and taking me with you on nature hikes; I've enjoyed those times greatly.

Those who have been faithful to stand with me in faith, God's faithful warriors: Ron, Ken, Denise, Isabel, Alanna, and Trish: I love you and thank the Lord for you. Jesus has given me His "best" intercessors and friends that His Kingdom has to offer. You are loved, and I know that Jesus has so much more to pour into your lives. Anita McCoy and Jane Blank: Keep fighting the "good fight of faith" and know that every promise God has made to you *will* be fulfilled! You are His faithful 11th hour workers.

To:

My "family" at *Discover Church* (formerly Oak Creek Assembly of God): You have blessed my life with your love and your encouragement, especially Pastor Brooks and Sherry. Your love and your kindness through the years have strengthened me to walk in the fullness that God has for my life. In this *new era* we will see countless miracles, salvations, and deliverances. I know, without a doubt, that the best days are right before us!

Darlene and Son Rise Ministries: Jesus has blessed you and has seen your faithfulness and your willingness to do His will above all. Get ready for the "overflow"; stand amazed and see what your God will do!

I give all the glory, honor, and praise to My Heavenly Father, to Jesus, and to the Holy Spirit for allowing me to write this book. Apart from You this book would never have been written. I dedicate this book to You and my entire life to Your service. My God, what a joy it is to love and to serve You! You are truly amazing!

Introduction

When you think of Mary, the mother of Jesus, what enters your mind? Do you think of people who bow before her statue in idolatrous worship? Or do you think of a young woman filled with faith and courage as she embraces the words of God concerning her destiny from the angel Gabriel? Mary was a woman of faith who embraced the call of God on her life. She was blessed because she believed that the Lord would fulfill His promises to her. (See Luke 1:45.)

In the Scriptures Mary never drew attention to herself; she would never draw attention away from Jesus, for she knew that He alone was and is the Savior of the world. She was a humble servant of God who submitted fully to the will of God. Mary was God's human vessel, a favored child of God, called to carry and to birth Jesus, but we must always remember: There is only *"One Mediator between God and men, the man Christ Jesus"* (1 Timothy 2:5 – King James Version).

This book is for all who desire to have a walk of overcoming faith... faith for the miraculous. Mary is set before us as an example of faith, trust, and full surrender to God's will, no matter the cost. I'm sure Mary didn't realize the full ramifications when she said "yes" to God's words spoken to her through the angel or how His word would be fulfilled; still she trusted the Lord above her own natural reasoning and understanding. Little did she realize the full cost of the pain and the suffering she would endure, but neither did she realize the extent of the divine favor and blessing that she would enjoy throughout eternity. God knew Mary's heart, and He knew her deep love for Him. The Lord knew that she would remain faithful to Him through all of the trials that she would go through because of her "yes."

This is the season, the decade of the miraculous, and those who have believed that the Lord would fulfill His promises to them will now be blessed beyond measure. Mary believed the words that Gabriel spoke to her concerning the conception and the birth of the Savior through her physical body, and now those who have surrendered all will "birth" the Son of God through their "spiritual wombs," the Life of Jesus. Out of their "bellies" will flow "rivers of living water" freeing multitudes from their captivity. (See John 7:38.) The Holy Spirit will flow through them bringing deliverance and refreshing to many who have been bound with generational iniquities, addictions, perversion, doubts, fears, and many other strongholds.

Mary's faith was tested greatly, but she stood firm through every fiery trial she faced. Mary positioned herself before God in faith and focused on His promises, knowing that God would surely fulfill her destiny in Him. She never lost sight of what God promised her, but she trusted His spoken word to her and overcame every obstacle that confronted her. It's no wonder that God called her "highly favored" through His angel. (See Luke 1:28.)

Truly she was blessed among women, but now all who have believed His Word, His promises to them in this hour, are "blessed" along with her. God has a company of Believers who have stood firm on His Word through many dark days of spiritual attacks and horrendous lies of the enemy. Like Mary they have stood on the promises of God even though in the natural it looked impossible for those promises to come to pass in their lives. These are the Lord's end-time "blessed ones" who have stood in faith against all odds and seemingly impossible situations. These are God's warriors of faith and trust, and they will stand with Mary on that final day and hear: *"Well done, good and faithful servant. You have been faithful over a little; I will set you over much. Enter into the joy of your master"* (Matthew 25:21b – English Standard Version). Wouldn't it be wonderful if others could look at our lives and say: *"Blessed is she who has believed that the Lord would fulfill what He has spoken to her"* (Luke 1:45 – Christian Standard Bible)?

Hear this word from God Almighty:

"Will you bend your will to Mine and surrender your all even when all you see before you are 'immovable mountains'? Can you believe Me as Mary did, lift your heart to Me in faith, and say: 'Behold the maidservant of the Lord! Let it be to me according to your word' (Luke 1:38b – New King James Version)? Can you believe My promises when everything in the natural looks contrary to what I have spoken to you?

"I am looking for a company of true Believers who will trust Me wholeheartedly and who will walk with Me in the realm of the miraculous...who will pay the cost and surrender all to Me in order for Me to fulfill My plan and My purpose for this nation and the nations of this world. Are you willing, My child? Are you willing to listen to My Spirit, to move out at My Word, and to believe Me for what looks impossible? Are you willing to lay down your life and to give Me every part of your heart and life, no matter the cost?

"I am waiting to hear your 'yes' so that I can overshadow you and bring forth the fullness of My Son within your spirit and soul...so that I can conform you fully into My image. As My Son is fully formed within you, I will then be able to move through you as My heart desires and set millions free from their chains and bondages. Give Me your heart, children, and let Me hear your 'yes,' for this is My will for you in this hour—says your God!"

Chapter 1
Mary: God's Woman of Faith

> Now in the sixth month the angel Gabriel was sent by God to a city of Galilee named Nazareth, to a virgin betrothed to a man whose name was Joseph, of the house of David. The virgin's name was Mary. And having come in, the angel said to her, "Rejoice, highly favored one, the Lord is with you; blessed are you among women!"
>
> –Luke 1:26–28

Mary was pledged to marry Joseph at a young age. According to Jewish cultural practices during this time, many young women were betrothed (engaged) as young as 12-years-old.[i] Many scholars believe that Mary was probably 14-years-old when the angel Gabriel visited her and gave her the news of being chosen to birth the Messiah, the Savior of the world.[i]

Mary was blessed and set apart among women in order to carry and to birth God's Son. This was not a random choice on God's part but a carefully planned decision in choosing Mary to be the mother of Jesus. She was highly favored and a "virgin" who had a pure heart before God. According to tradition derived from certain apocryphal writings found in the 2nd century, *Protevangelium of James*, Anne and Joachim were Mary's parents.[ii] This is a noncanonical source, so no one is sure if this is factual.[ii] Though we don't have details concerning this, I believe that Mary was well-versed in Scripture and that her parents taught her about the love and the power of God. (See Luke 1:47–55.) We can know that Mary was raised by godly parents who influenced her life greatly; we can see this by her response to Gabriel in her glorious visitation.

> But when she saw him, she was troubled at his saying, and considered what manner of greeting this was. Then the angel said to her, "Do not be afraid, Mary, for you have found favor with God. And behold, you will conceive in your womb and bring forth a Son, and shall call His name JESUS. He will be great, and will be called the Son of the Highest; and the Lord God will give Him the throne of His father David. And He will reign over the house of Jacob forever, and of His kingdom there will be no end." Then Mary said to the angel, "How can this be, since I do not know a man?" And the angel answered and said to her, "The Holy Spirit will come upon you, and the power of the Highest will overshadow you; therefore, also, that Holy One who is to be born will be called the Son of God. Now indeed, Elizabeth your relative has also conceived a son in her old age; and this is now the sixth month for her who was called barren. For with God nothing will be impossible." Then Mary said, "Behold the maidservant of the Lord! Let it be to me according to your word." And the angel departed from her.
>
> –Luke 1:29–38

Though Mary was young her faith and trust in God was strong. She believed but was "troubled" because of the angel's spoken words to her. I'm sure she felt humbled and even startled by this unexpected visit from God's angel. Mary was a simple, humble child of God, one who prayed and sought the Lord. But to have a visitation like this, I'm sure it overwhelmed her! She must have thought to herself: *"Why am I highly favored and blessed among women?"* She must have been in shock when the angel told her that she would bring forth God's Son! Her natural mind wondered: *How in the world will I have a child when I am a virgin and do not know a man?* She questioned the angel about this, but it was not in a spirit of unbelief. This was her natural mind and reasoning that kicked into gear, but when the angel told her that the Holy Spirit would come upon her and the power of the Highest would overshadow her, she just accepted and believed His word without fully understanding how this would come about. Then when the angel revealed that Elizabeth, her relative, was pregnant in her old age, it strengthened her faith, and she knew that nothing was impossible for this mighty God!

How would you feel or react if an angel had made such a glorious announcement to you? Would you be troubled? Would you question why you were chosen to fulfill such a glorious destiny and calling in your life? I know I would have been shocked by this visitation!

What about the promises that God has spoken to you personally? Are you believing that these promises will come to pass in God's perfect timing? Are you fighting "the good fight of faith?" (See 1 Timothy 6:12.) Have you closed your ears to the lies of the enemy telling you that they will never come to pass? Remember: The Lord <u>will</u> fulfill His promises to us, for He is faithful and worthy of our trust! (See Genesis 28:15.)

> And Mary said, "My soul magnifies and exalts the Lord, and my spirit has rejoiced in God my Savior. For He has looked [with loving care] on the humble state of His maidservant; for behold, from now on all generations will count me blessed and happy and favored by God! For He who is mighty has done great things for me; and holy is His name [to be worshiped in His purity, majesty, and glory]. AND HIS MERCY IS UPON GENERATION AFTER GENERATION TOWARD THOSE WHO [stand in great awe of God and] FEAR HIM."
> –Luke 1:46–50 – Amplified Bible

Mary knew that she needed a Savior, someone to save her from her sin and weaknesses. She felt her weakness and desperate need for God, but she also knew that she was blessed and highly favored. God did not choose someone who was sinless or flawless but someone who felt and knew her desperate need for Him. Mary leaned hard on her God, for she knew that apart from Him she could do nothing. Her eyes and her focus were on the Lord alone, not on her own strength or ability. She knew, like the apostle Paul, that when she was weak the Lord was strong in her. (See 2 Corinthians

12:9–10.) The Lord was her strength and her song, but the Lord knew she would need a godly man who would help and uphold her through all that she would go through. God sent her Joseph, a man hand-picked by the Lord for her to lean on as she walked out God's plan and purpose for her life and to be the earthly father and godly influence, along with Mary, in Jesus' life.

Mary was not only a woman of faith and trust but a woman who knew how to worship her God! She rejoiced in God her Savior and stood firm in faith throughout her life, though I'm sure she had many ups and downs. She never wavered in her faith and trust in God but was steady on the narrow path that the Lord had placed her on. Mary was filled with great awe in what the angel revealed to her. She truly walked in the fear of the Lord. Her whole life was fully committed to accomplish her heavenly Father's will. I believe that she continually grew in her faith and had to stand against unbelief many times. She was a woman who learned how to walk in the miraculous!

> Joseph, to whom she was engaged, was a righteous man and did not want to disgrace her publicly, so he decided to break the engagement quietly. As he considered this, an angel of the Lord appeared to him in a dream. "Joseph, son of David," the angel said, "do not be afraid to take Mary as your wife. For the child within her was conceived by the Holy Spirit. And she will have a son, and you are to name Him Jesus, for He will save His people from their sins." All of this occurred to fulfill the Lord's message through His prophet: "Look! The virgin will conceive a child! She will give birth to a son, and they will call Him Immanuel, which means 'God is with us.'" When Joseph woke up, he did as the angel of the Lord commanded and took Mary as his wife.
> –Matthew 1:19–24 – New Living Translation

Joseph was gentle yet strong in his faith and open to receive whatever God would reveal to him. When we see how he handled this situation concerning Mary, we realize that he was a righteous man, full of integrity and obedient to the Lord's will for his life. No wonder God chose him to be the earthly father of Jesus! Think of the pain and the confusion that Joseph must have gone through when he discovered Mary was pregnant. This was a painful, fiery trial for this man of God. Still, he did not want to disgrace her publicly. He wanted to "cover her shame" and break his engagement with her quietly.

The Lord knew that He needed to assure Joseph concerning Mary's pregnancy, so an angel of the Lord appeared to him in a dream and reassured him that Mary's pregnancy was supernatural and that she would birth God's Son. In this visitation the angel quoted the Old Testament verse Isaiah 7:14 to confirm this truth and to encourage Joseph. This man is highly honored in Heaven for His faithful obedience to the Father's will. This wasn't Joseph's only visitation, for when times of danger came God warned him in dreams, and Joseph would immediately obey. (See Matthew 2:13–15, 19–22.) Let's honor this faithful servant of God, for he, along with Mary, was chosen and highly favored by the Lord; he also believed the words that were spoken to him.

> In those days Mary arose and went with haste into the hill country, to a town in Judah, and she entered the house of Zechariah and greeted Elizabeth. And when Elizabeth heard the greeting of Mary, the baby leaped in her womb. And Elizabeth was filled with the Holy Spirit, and she exclaimed with a loud cry, "Blessed are you among women, and blessed is the fruit of your womb! And why is this granted to me that the mother of my Lord should come to me? For behold, when the sound of your greeting came to my ears, the baby in my womb leaped for joy. **And blessed is she who believed that there would be a fulfillment of what was spoken to her from the Lord.**"
> –Luke 1:39–45 – ESV, emphasis added

There were several reasons, I believe, that Mary made haste to see Elizabeth. She wanted to rejoice with her relative's "miraculous" pregnancy, miraculous because Elizabeth was past child bearing age, and help her as she neared the birthing of her child. I also believe that Mary felt that

Elizabeth would believe and rejoice with her when she shared her visitation from the angel Gabriel and what was spoken to her. Mary wanted someone she could open her heart to and know that she wouldn't be ridiculed, and Elizabeth was the one relative she could do this with. Elizabeth was a woman of faith, and how thrilled Mary must have been when she spoke prophetically to her even before Mary told her the good news! Mary must have marveled at what Elizabeth spoke concerning her, and it confirmed the words that were spoken to her by the angel. I'm sure this confirmation strengthened her faith and trust in God.

Elizabeth's husband, Zechariah, also had a glorious visitation from an angel 6 months before the angel appeared to Mary, but Zechariah did <u>not</u> believe the words that the angel Gabriel spoke to him. So, because of his unbelief, the angel told him that he would not be able to speak until the time when the words spoken to Zechariah would be fulfilled. (See Luke 1:5–23.)

Unbelief in the promises of God will always silence our testimony, but faith in God's promises always brings great blessings. I believe Zechariah grew in faith when Elizabeth became pregnant, and his faith continued to grow throughout the months of her pregnancy. I believe that by the time the baby was born, his faith was strong. He must have repented deeply before God for his unbelief. In God's grace Zechariah's faith and trust in His promises was restored.

The angel told Zechariah to name his son John, and after his season of silence he demonstrated his faith by confirming that his son was to be named John, even after his relatives wanted to name him Zechariah after him. When he asked for a writing tablet and wrote, "His name is John," his mouth was immediately opened, and his tongue was set free, and he began to speak, praising God. (See Luke 1:59–64.)

I believe that we will see something similar in this generation. Many who have not believed in the promises of God will repent deeply before the Lord for their unbelief. As God moves in strength and in power and begins to release the fullness of His glory and power in this generation, millions will bow low before the Lord, and God will release their tongues. Millions of captives, those who have been bound with fear and unbelief, will praise Him with great shouts of joy as their tongues are set free!

The Lord will restore their faith as He did Zechariah's, for without faith it is impossible to please God. (See Hebrews 11:6.)

> Take care, brothers and sisters, that there will not be in any one of you an evil, unbelieving heart that falls away from the living God. But encourage one another every day, as long as it is still called "today," so that none of you will be hardened by the deceitfulness of sin. For we have become partakers of Christ if we keep the beginning of our commitment firm until the end, while it is said, "TODAY IF YOU HEAR HIS VOICE, DO NOT HARDEN YOUR HEARTS, AS WHEN THEY PROVOKED ME." For who provoked Him when they had heard? Indeed, did not all those who came out of Egypt led by Moses? And with whom was He angry for forty years? Was it not with those who sinned, whose dead bodies fell in the wilderness? And to whom did He swear that they would not enter His rest, but to those who were disobedient? **And so we see that they were not able to enter because of unbelief.**
> –Hebrews 3:12–19 – New American Standard Bible, emphasis added

A few years ago God showed me that there are 2 main "strongholds" in the lives of His children: **unbelief and fear.** Jesus revealed to me that the 2 "central pillars" that Samson stood between could be likened to these 2 strongholds that have been holding millions captive, and that now, in this very hour, these pillars are going to come crashing down and God is going to free His children from these demonic chains. (See Judges 16:28–30.)

In spiritual warfare God's true children have been pushing against these 2 "central pillars" every time fear and unbelief would come against them, and through this warfare they have developed strong spiritual "wings." When God's children would push these pillars down, they would spring back up as the enemy would come against them again and again. God showed me in the Spirit that these 2 pillars, one on each side of His people, have been pushed down and have sprung back up so quickly and so many times that these pillars have actually turned into "spiritual wings."

Because of this continual warfare God's warrior children have become so spiritually strong that they will now begin to soar with Him to new and glorious heights in the Spirit. Because of this spiritual strength that has been developed in His people, these 2 pillars, these 2 strongholds will now break completely off of their lives. These pillars, these strongholds have been so weakened that they will now completely collapse! These pillars of fear and unbelief must be crushed if we are to have *faith for the miraculous!*

> For in Christ Jesus neither circumcision nor uncircumcision avails anything, but faith working through love.
> –Galatians 5:6 – NKJV

Faith works through love; without love we will never have faith to *walk in the miraculous.* If our hearts are filled with fear, unbelief, hate, and unforgiveness, the Spirit will not be able to flow through us in the miraculous. Only as we release all bitterness and open our hearts fully to the love of Christ will we experience the miracles that our hearts so long for. Only as we abide in Christ and He abides in us can we know His love and miracle-working power, for apart from Him we can do nothing. (See John 15:4–7.) We must eat the "Living Bread" from Heaven, Jesus, if we are to be partakers of the divine nature of Jesus. (See John 6:51.) Only as we receive the love of God and know Him intimately in our hearts and lives can we be completely freed from fear and unbelief, for the perfect love of God casts out all fear. (See 1 John 4:18.) So many know Jesus only in their natural minds but not in their hearts as a "Living Savior." Knowledge will not free us fully, but His love and power will!

For most of my life I struggled with fear and unbelief because of past trauma, but as I grew in the knowledge and understanding of my Father's love for me, fear began to leave. Spending precious hours with Jesus, eating and drinking in not only His Word but His very life and love for me, loosened those heavy chains from my soul, and they began to fall off of my life. I longed to be free; I longed to have *faith for the miraculous,* but only as I exercised my faith through God's Word against the enemy, only as I received the love of My heavenly Father and released unforgiveness from my heart, only then did I begin to see the miraculous begin to take place in my life.

It is not enough to have head knowledge; faith must be released from the heart. We can quote a thousand Scriptures, but if we do not have a "living faith" and relationship with Jesus, we will never reach the heights of glory that the Spirit longs to bring us into. Only Christ's living faith "birthed" in our souls can bring us into the realm of the miraculous. Only as we plant God's "seeds of faith," His Word, in our hearts and nourish these "seeds" in prayer and in obedience to His will, will we grow and see our lives become fruitful for our King. We will then walk hand-in-hand with our Savior, and He will reveal His miraculous power in and through our lives.

There will be times in our lives when the Lord will show us that we have grown spiritually. I have known much demonic warfare throughout my life, and many times I cringed before the enemy because I saw him as a giant. But as I grew in my love relationship with Jesus and came to know the deep love of my Father, I began to see the enemy as the "grasshopper" that he truly is. One night around midnight I got up for a little while and then went back to bed. As I began to doze off, I felt the evil presence of a demon of fear. Immediately, my spirit-man rose up, and I came against this spirit twice with the blood of Jesus. I then said: *"And don't you ever come back."* I was in a twilight sleep, but my spirit-man rose up in great power and authority. It was wonderful to see where the Lord had brought me. No more fear of the enemy, for now I know who I am in Christ. This is where God wants to bring each one of His children in this hour; this is the place where we will find the faith that we need to walk in the miraculous!

God desires to make His people a source of joy and pleasure to His heart, and this happens when we allow the Spirit to move upon us and to overshadow us with His presence and His love. God desires us to be conformed fully into the image of His Son. (See Romans 8:29.) This brings the Lord great joy. When we truly believe the words that God speaks to us, we will then have *faith to walk in the miraculous.* This is God's will and desire for each one of His children, and I pray we would be willing to say "yes" to all that the Lord speaks to us, no matter the cost.

The Lord has kept a faithful remnant strong in this hour. They have stood on His Word through many storms, and even as Mary birthed the Son of God physically, they will "birth" God's Son, spiritually, and will bear much fruit in this hour. The Lord's faithful ones are a blessed company of true Believers who have believed God's spoken words to them; they are true children of faith along with Mary, and they will never be silenced!

Overshadowed by the Holy Spirit – The Seed of Christ

What does it mean to be overshadowed? According to HELPS Word-studies: "**1982** *episkiázō* (from 1909 /*epí*, 'upon' and *skiazō*, 'to cast shade') – properly, to cast a shadow *on;* overshadow, which leaves a natural (apt) result. 1982 /*episkiázō* ('overshadow') is used in the NT of *God's overshadowing presence* – which always brings His *boulē*-plan to pass (see 1012 /*boulḗ*, 'God's immutable will for *physical circumstances*')."[iii]

From God's Word we read that the Holy Spirit "overshadowed" Mary, and with His "shadow," His very presence, He accomplished His will by planting the "seed of Christ" inside Mary's physical womb. (See Luke 1:35.) This was a wonder-working miracle that literally brought forth the life-seed of His Son, Jesus. God accomplished His immutable will and brought forth the physical circumstances that He desired in Mary's life and for all of mankind. What a miracle-working God!

In much the same way when we come to Christ and surrender to Him fully, the "seed of Christ" is planted inside our "spiritual womb," and as we yield to the Spirit the Life of Christ then begins to be formed in us and to flow through us in the power of the Spirit. Out of our "belly" these waters of Life begin to flow through us. (See John 7:38.) This is the life of Jesus, not our own goodness, not our own power, but His alone.

> For those whom He foreknew [and loved and chose beforehand], He also predestined to be **conformed to the image of His Son** [and ultimately share in His complete

sanctification], so that He would be the firstborn [the most beloved and honored] among many believers.

–Romans 8:29 – AMP, emphasis added

God desires to sanctify us fully and to set us apart in this hour for His plan and His purpose in the earth to be fulfilled. It is God who is at work in us to will and to do of His good pleasure. (See Philippians 2:13.) In our own strength and power we cannot change ourselves in the deep places within our souls. Only the Holy Spirit can transform us from the inside out. The Lord is asking us to yield to Him fully in this hour and to allow His Holy Fire to make the changes in us that He desires.

This is the meaning of the parable: The seed is the Word of God.

–Luke 8:11 – New International Version

In the beginning was the Word, and the Word was with God, and the Word was God.

–John 1:1 – NKJV

Having been born again, not of corruptible seed but incorruptible, through the Word of God which lives and abides forever.

–1 Peter 1:23

The "seed" that was planted in us when we "received" Christ into our hearts and lives needs to be nourished daily through His Word, His very presence. Jesus is the "Living Word" inside of us, and only in Him can we come to full spiritual maturity. We have been born of the Spirit, the incorruptible "seed of Christ" through the Word of God. Only in Jesus can Eternal Life be found as we receive all that He has for our lives. As the Holy Spirit overshadows us, it is then, and only then, that the Life of Jesus enters our spiritual womb, and we begin to grow into the fullness of Christ.

There is a great deception in the Church that tells a sinner that if they say a prayer they can be saved and born-again. No soul can be saved apart from the work of the Holy Spirit drawing them, convicting them of sin, and planting the "seed of Christ" within their spirit. This is a sovereign work of the Holy Spirit. We are called to preach and to teach the Truth of the Gospel, but only God can save a soul. There are many, many false conversions in the Church…souls that truly need to have a *true* encounter with the living Christ. Only the Spirit can plant the seed of Christ into the seeking soul.

After our true salvation experience the Holy Spirit will then come and nourish the seed of Christ, His Word, within us, and the glorious work of being conformed into the image of Christ can begin. As we grow and mature in the Lord, He will then be able to remove every obstacle and will flow through our lives unhindered. This is the true "born-again" experience: the fullness of Christ living and flowing through our lives. Unless we are born-again we will not see or walk in Kingdom power and authority. Man can never save himself, for that which is born of the flesh is flesh and that which is born of the Spirit is Spirit. (See John 3:3–8.)

> Everyone who is truly God's child will refuse to keep sinning because God's seed remains within him, and he is unable to continue sinning because he has been fathered by God Himself.
>
> –1 John 3:9 – The Passion Translation

We have been "fathered" by God; we have His very nature, His DNA, and this is something that only the Spirit of God can release in our lives. We are His children if we have truly been born from on High. Many have religion; many have a church membership, but that does not make them a child of God. We must be overshadowed by the Spirit of God and have His "Holy Seed" planted in us or we will never SEE the Kingdom of God! The nature of Christ must abide in us, for only then will sin no longer have dominion over us. (See Romans 6:14.) We must examine our lives to see if we are truly in the faith. (See 2 Corinthians 13:5.) If we see little or no change **in** our lives…if we see little or no spiritual fruit being released **through** our lives, we need to run to Jesus and cry out to Him and allow the Spirit to show us our hearts and change us from the inside out.

> Yea, though I walk through the valley of the shadow of death, I will fear no evil; for Thou art with me; Thy rod and Thy staff, they comfort me.
> –Psalm 23:4 – American Standard Version

There will be times when we will walk through the valley of the "shadow of death," but we can know that we are overshadowed by the Holy Spirit and that we have nothing to fear. No evil will touch us, for we are safe in His loving arms. His rod protects us from our enemies, and His staff will guide us and keep us on the narrow path that He has us on. He is our comfort as we go through pain and difficulty. Jesus is our faithful and loving Shepherd.

> He who dwells in the shelter of the Most High will remain secure and rest in the Shadow of the Almighty [whose power no enemy can withstand].
> –Psalm 91:1 – AMP

> How precious is Your lovingkindness, O God! The children of men take refuge in the shadow of Your wings.
> –Psalm 36:7

> As he was saying these things, a cloud came and overshadowed them, and they were afraid as they entered the cloud. And a voice came out of the cloud, saying, "This is My Son, My Chosen One; listen to Him!" And when the voice had spoken, Jesus was found alone.
> –Luke 9:34–36a – ESV

The disciples were afraid when God overshadowed them, and this is a common experience for anyone who encounters God in this way. When you are overshadowed and the Lord draws near to you, you sense His holiness and power, and you may even tremble in His presence. When the Lord draws you close in the "secret place" of communion with Him, you will then begin to hear His voice more clearly, and you will focus on Jesus alone. Hearing His voice clearly and seeing "only Him" will be your experience as you spend time with Jesus daily in prayer and in His Word. This is something that can be developed in your life as you discipline your life before Him. As we are overshadowed by the Spirit, we will hear the voice of the Father saying: *"This is My Son, My Chosen One; listen to Him!"* Spending time with the Lord brings us to the place of enjoying and delighting in Him above all the joys and pleasures of this world. We will delight to not only hear His voice but also to obey Him in all things!

> But to all who believed Him and accepted Him, He gave the right to become children of God. They are reborn—not with a physical birth resulting from human passion or plan, but a birth that comes from God.
>
> –John 1:12–13 – NLT

These "reborn" children of faith who have received the "incorruptible seed" of Jesus will now bring forth out of their "spiritual wombs" the life of Jesus. Christ has been fully formed within them, and they are ready to birth. They are positioned and ready to bring forth from their lives all that God desires. They are focused on doing the Father's will above all, and they will not be moved, come hell or high water. They are a fierce company of warriors who will now be released to show forth the wonders of God. Get ready to hear their "roars," their cries, as they birth God's purposes into the earth!

The Spirit would say:

> *"I have 'overshadowed' you with My love and presence, and in this shadow of My glory you will be safe. No harm will come to you, for I will keep you safe in the 'haven' of My love. Though it looks dark at times, know that I am doing a transforming work in your soul. I am removing 'strong-holds' that have kept you in a prison of fear and doubt.*
>
> *"Never fear when My cloud of glory descends upon you, for it is here, in the refuge of My arms, that you will come to know*

Me in ways that will astound you. You will hear My voice and see Me face to face, and you will never fear again. All other loves will fade away, and the things of this earth will grow 'strangely dim.'

"Trust Me in this powerful 'overshadowing' that you are experiencing, for the Life of My Son is being formed inside of you, and you will come forth as pure gold. Like Mary you will have a song of praise, and it will fill the heavens and the earth, and all who hear it will stand in awe as they see My glory and power resting upon you. Your life will be forever changed and transformed even as a caterpillar transforms into a butterfly, and you will soar with Me in freedom and joy.

"Come; allow My Spirit to finish this work in your soul, and do not despise the discipline of the Father, for whom the Lord loves, He disciplines. (See Hebrews 12:4–11.) Did I tell you this would be easy? Didn't I tell you that the gate is narrow and the road hard? (See Matthew 7:13–14.) Why do you look for earthly pleasures to satisfy your soul? Only I, the Lord your God, will satisfy you fully. You belong to Me, not to this world. This world will never fully satisfy you. Only in My arms, as I overshadow you, will you come to that place of rest and experience the comfort of My love that you so long for.

"So come; come close to Me, closer than you ever have before, and don't be afraid. These 'dark clouds' that have covered your life are filled with glory and power. These 'dark clouds' are transforming your soul, and you will come to the place where you will see only Me. This is your hearts deepest longing: to see Me, to know My intimate embrace, and to be free from the 'shackles' that have bound you for so long.

"Come to Me, and you will know My plan for your life: an adventure of glory and power that you have never experienced. I have so much for you, children; deny Me no longer; surrender fully to the work of My Spirit within you. Allow My Spirit to overshadow you and to make those internal changes within your soul so that you can soar with Me in this season. Know that I love and care for you more than any earthly parent ever could.

You are 'engraved on the palm of My hand.' (See Isaiah 49:16.) You are Mine—says your God!"

It's Time to Birth!

"Shout for joy, infertile one, you who have not given birth to any child; break forth into joyful shouting and cry aloud, you who have not been in labor; for the sons of the desolate one will be more numerous than the sons of the married woman," says the LORD. "Enlarge the place of your tent; stretch out the curtains of your dwellings, do not spare them; lengthen your ropes and strengthen your pegs. For you will spread out to the right and to the left. And your descendants will possess nations and will resettle the desolate cities. Fear not, for you will not be put to shame; and do not feel humiliated, for you will not be disgraced; but you will forget the shame of your youth, and no longer remember the disgrace of your widowhood. For your husband is your Maker, whose name is the LORD of armies; and your Redeemer is the Holy One of Israel, who is called the God of all the earth."
–Isaiah 54:1–5 – NASB

This is the season when many are "birthing" God's purposes into the earth. Can you hear the sound of joyful shouting from those who have suffered many "barren" years and have seen little fruit in their lives but are now realizing great fruitfulness in the Spirit? This is the time of the great turn-around when many that have been "hidden" and have suffered long delays and seeming setbacks in their lives will now "birth" Jesus fully in their lives.

There are many of God's people that feel as if they will never be fruitful for the Lord. They have not won many souls for Jesus neither have they experienced a fruitful ministry. They have been in the "secret place" with Jesus for years, travailing in prayer and seeking Him with their whole heart. They have wept before Him until they felt they had no more tears to weep. Many of God's "desolate" ones have forgotten God's Word which states in Psalm 126:5–6 (TPT): *"Those who sow their tears as seeds will reap a harvest with joyful shouts of glee. They may weep as they go out carrying their seed to sow, but they will return with joyful laughter and shouting with gladness as they bring back armloads of blessing and a harvest overflowing!"*

We see here that tears are like "seeds" that will eventually bring forth an overflowing harvest of blessing and an overflowing harvest of souls. God takes our tears and uses them, I believe, to soften those who have hard, stony hearts. Those who have allowed the Spirit to break them and to pour His life through them in travail and in tears will return from their barrenness and desolation with untold blessings and will "birth" many souls into the Kingdom of God. None of our tears or trials are in vain, and in God's perfect timing we will see much "fruit" and realize that our "season of barrenness" was only preparing us for a greater harvest of fruitfulness.

God is stretching and enlarging our hearts so that we can contain more of His love and glory. This stretching of our "tent," our hearts and lives, will widen our spiritual territory and influence in ways that will astound us. Spiritual "stretching" involves pain, and in order to have influence and authority in the Spirit, we must go through many spiritual "exercises" that will "stretch" our faith and make us pliable in the hand of the "Master Potter." We must go through many painful trials in order to not only understand the pain that others are going through but to empathize and weep with them.

Jesus has not destined us for shame, humiliation, and disgrace, and though we may feel shame for a season because of our past, God will heal our wounds and remove all of the shame and grief with His love for us. We may have felt the disgrace of spiritual "widowhood" for a season, but after the storms we will know our Maker as our "Husband." There will not be one need in our lives that will remain unmet as we surrender and yield ourselves fully to Him. He is our Protector, our Love, our Strength, our Peace, our Joy, our Provider, our Comforter, and our All in All! All we could ever want or need will be found in our Beloved Jesus.

> That is why my body is full of trembling. Pain grips me like the pain of childbirth. I'm disturbed by what I hear. I'm terrified by what I see.
> –Isaiah 21:3 – God's Word Translation

Pregnancy, labor, and childbirth in the natural realm is the perfect comparison of what "spiritual birthing" is in the spiritual realm, but in the Spirit this process may take much longer than 9 months. In the natural as a baby grows within the mother's womb, there will be days of weariness and internal pressure. She may grow impatient and wonder if the time of delivery will ever come. It may be hard as the baby grows within the womb to find a comfortable position in bed and even in sitting. Fears may assail her, wondering if the baby is healthy, and anxiety about the pain of childbirth, for she knows that when the time of labor comes there will be intense pain if she is delivering the baby naturally.

In the same way as we are being conformed into Christ's image, we will experience days of intense internal pressure because of the spiritual warfare that may come against us. During this season of spiritual growth, we may grow weary, spiritually and physically, because of this intense work inside of our souls. We may grow impatient and wonder if we will ever come out of the "fiery crucible" that Jesus has us in. There will be times when we will feel very uncomfortable because of what is being exposed in our hearts and lives, but as we run to the "God of all comfort," He will fill us with His love and joy, and Jesus will remove every fear that we may have in our hearts concerning the "birth" of our "destiny child."

Sometimes we may need encouragement during this process as I did with my 3rd child. An angel came and stood at the foot of my bed and said: *"God is with you, and you will come through this storm quickly."* This 3rd labor and delivery was much harder than my first 2 pregnancies, and God knew that I needed comfort. My husband was with me when this angel came into the room, but when I asked him if he saw the "man" that came into my room, he said: *"No man ever came into your room."* Truly, God is the God of all comfort!

Many times when the Spirit is working in the depths of our heart, we feel pain, grief, and fear, but we must realize that this is all a part of the process of "birthing" Christ within our spirit, soul, and bodies. Even as Mary felt labor pains in birthing Jesus through her physical body so will we travail as we bring forth the life of Jesus inside of our hearts and lives. Sometimes terror grips our lives when we go through the "dark night of the soul," but this must happen if we are to enjoy the fullness of Christ in our lives. There may be times when we are "disturbed" by what we experience as God takes us through deep waters, but know that everything you go through in Jesus is not in vain. You may not see the outcome of what God has promised you yet, but in God's perfect timing you will.

> My little children, for whom I am again in [the pains of] labor until Christ is [completely and permanently] formed within you.
> –Galatians 4:19 – AMP

"Birthing" in the Spirit is not a *female* experience only; I know of many men that carried the fullness of Christ and travailed to bring forth His plans and purposes into the earth…men of passion and power who knew how to get ahold of Heaven for themselves and others. I believe God is raising up true "fathers of faith" in this season who will mentor many of God's people and bring them to full maturity in Christ.

Not only did the Apostle Paul know what it was like to travail in the Spirit but so did Isaiah and Elijah. (See 1 Kings 18:42; Isaiah 21:3.) I think of King David and the heart-felt Psalms that he wrote. David truly knew what it was to weep and to travail before his God! Hear his heart of intercession in Psalm 6:6–9 (TPT): *"I'm worn out with my weeping and groaning. Night after night I soak my pillow with tears, and flood my bed with weeping. My eyes of faith won't focus anymore, for sorrow fills my heart. There are so many enemies who come against me! Turn from me, all you troublemakers! For Yahweh has turned to hear the sound of my weeping. Yes! Yahweh my healer has heard all my pleading and has taken hold of my prayers and answered them all."*

True intercessors in Christ have known what it is like to spend much time in the "secret place" travailing before the Lord: weeping, crying out, and experiencing the depths of Jesus' heart for the lost and the dying.

This "birthing" is not something you can experience in your own power or strength or "work up" through your flesh.

I remember one time as a young Believer I went to a Christian crusade at the Milwaukee arena. I was led to go to the prayer room where God's people were gathered for prayer. As I knelt the Spirit of God came upon me, and I began to travail deeply. This was an unexpected but powerful experience. Others gathered around me and laid hands on me and prayed. I don't remember how long I travailed, but when the Spirit lifted His burden from my soul, I knew that something supernatural had been accomplished. The Lord had His way through all the intercessors that prayed in the Spirit that day, and I believe many souls were saved and set free. You do not have to be 40-years-old, spiritually, to experience the travail of the Spirit; you only need to be yielded and available and allow the Spirit to do what He wants through your "vessel."

> A woman giving birth to a child has pain because her time has come; but when her baby is born she forgets the anguish because of her joy that a child is born into the world. So with you: Now is your time of grief, but I will see you again and you will rejoice, and no one will take away your joy. In that day you will no longer ask Me anything. Very truly I tell you, My Father will give you whatever you ask in My name. Until now you have not asked for anything in My name. Ask and you will receive, and your joy will be complete.
> –John 16:21–24 – NIV

There is always pain in giving birth, whether physically or spiritually, but when we experience the joy of "birthing" our "destiny child," we will rejoice with joy unspeakable and full of glory! I believe every true child of God has a destiny "seed" within them, and we are called to nourish and to protect this "child" until the fullness of our calling comes forth. We will forget the anguish of our trials and rejoice in the fullness and glory that God has planned for our lives, and no one will ever again take this joy from us. This is the season of "birthing" and receiving all that our Heavenly Father has for us. Because we have believed that the

Lord would fulfill His promises to us, we are blessed, along with Mary, and our joy will be complete!

If you desire to learn more on "birthing" in the Spirit, I go into much more detail in my book: **Called to Travail: Birthing God's End Time Purposes into the Earth.**

Listen to God's words of life:

> *"This has been an intense season of 'birthing' My purposes into the earth. The warfare has been intense but so has the outpouring of My glory and power. No darkness can stop what your Almighty King is 'birthing' into the earth.*
>
> *"Now is the time and season, the decade of glory that I have promised you. My children are coming forth in great power and authority, and they are taking the 'Land.' They are moving with My promises, and they are believing Me for impossible situations to turn-around for My glory. Yesterday is gone for them, and they have stepped into a new day with Me.*
>
> *"So come forth, My bride, and 'birth' the fullness of My plans and purposes for this generation and for this earth. Now you will see the miraculous power of the Lord your God. You have labored and travailed for years in My Spirit, and now the fullness of My Son is coming forth from your life. I have heard your cries, and I have seen your tears for many years, My beloved, and now I am taking those tears and pouring them upon this earth to awaken a multitude of souls—all for My glory. These 'seeds' you have planted will no longer lie dormant, for they are now springing forth into new life within your soul, your spirit, and your body.*
>
> *"Many will now be awakened to their true identity in Me and will no longer cower before the enemy of their soul. Great healings will now come forth, and those who have 'sown in tears' will now reap great joy and a harvest of righteousness that will astound many. (See Psalm 126:5.) This is the time and season for My recompense to come forth, and what the enemy has stolen will now be returned 7-fold. Watch and see now what I will do. I will awaken millions upon millions of souls and breathe upon*

the 'dead dry bones' that have been bound by the evil one for many years.

"Birth, My bride, birth, and bring forth the fullness of My Son through your life. Release the power and the glory of My Son through your 'vessel' and **see** now the glory...**experience** now the power that you have so long awaited for. Don't be afraid to move with My Spirit into the 'unknown' future that is before you, for it is not unknown to Me. The path that I have ordained you to walk on in this hour will be new and exciting with many 'twists and turns,' but know that all of this has been foreordained for your life.

"As the life of My Son comes forth from you now, you will know what you have been created for, and I promise you: You will fulfill your calling and destiny, and no one, nothing will stop you from finishing your earthly race in My Son—says your God!"

Chapter 2

A Living Sacrifice: Holy and Acceptable

And so, dear brothers and sisters, I plead with you to give your bodies to God because of all He has done for you. Let them be a living and holy sacrifice—the kind He will find acceptable. This is truly the way to worship Him. Don't copy the behavior and customs of this world, but let God transform you into a new person by changing the way you think. Then you will learn to know God's will for you, which is good and pleasing and perfect.
–Romans 12:1-2 – NLT

I love this verse in the NLT version; I believe it more fully expresses the heart of Jesus for this generation. Paul was "pleading" with his brothers and sisters in Christ to give themselves fully to the Lord, to give Him everything, even their very bodies. This is the heart of God for all of His children in this hour: to seek *first* the Kingdom of God and His righteousness and to let go of all of the things of this world, its ways and its customs. (See Matthew 6:33.) I believe that in these past 2 years the Spirit of God has been helping us to do this in the midst of all the darkness and the chaos around us. We have seen and experienced that our stability is found in Christ alone, the "Rock" of our salvation.

Paul is one of the greatest examples of surrendering his body, his spirit, and his soul to Jesus. Paul went through scourgings, shipwrecks, being beaten with rods, stonings, and all manner of physical suffering along with all of his internal pain through betrayals, misunderstandings, and rejections. Paul gave his everything to the Spirit of God, and because of this he was able to write at least 13 books in the New Testament. The Lord was able to use him in dramatic ways in bringing souls to Christ, releasing healing power, and encouraging the Body of Christ. (See Acts 19:11–12.) Paul's body was proof that he was a servant of the Lord. He held nothing back.

> From now on let no one trouble me [by making it necessary for me to justify my authority as an apostle, and the absolute truth of the gospel], for I bear on my body the branding-marks of Jesus [the wounds, scars, and other outward evidence of persecutions—these testify to His ownership of me].
> –Galatians 6:17 – AMP

Mary also gave her body, her entire life to God when she said "yes" to her calling and her destiny in Him. Her surrender to God's will allowed her to carry and to birth the Son of God in her physical body, but I believe that most of Mary's scars and wounds were internal, in her heart and soul, as she walked out her destiny in the Lord. Even though Mary had a few people that believed she was carrying God's Son, they only believed because of a divine revelation or an angelic dream; most of the people around her did not believe she was carrying the Messiah. Even Joseph was ready to divorce her quietly until an angel appeared to him in a dream and confirmed her pregnancy was Spirit-conceived. (See Matthew 1:19–23.)

Mary let go of her life fully and unconditionally in order to fulfill her destiny, and this is what God is calling His people to do in this very hour. Jesus is calling us into His rest…to cease from our own works and to yield to His Spirit, no matter the cost. As "living sacrifices" Jesus is calling us to live a selfless life of obedience, for only then will He accept our worship. Many believe that if they sing loud enough during a worship service that this is pleasing to God. They worship in song then leave the service to live their own lives and do their "own thing." The Lord will not accept worship from hearts that are bent on planning their own lives according to their natural reasoning and doing whatever they please. Jesus calls this rebellion and idolatry. (See Matthew 7:21–23; 1 Samuel 15:23; 1 John 2:15–17.) We can do all kinds of good works, but if they are not Spirit-birthed they will burn up before us on Judgment Day.

> For no one can lay a foundation other than the one which is [already] laid, which is Jesus Christ. But if anyone builds on the foundation with gold, silver, precious stones, wood, hay, straw, each one's work will be clearly shown [for what it is]; for the day [of judgment] will disclose it, because it is to be revealed with fire, and the fire will test the quality and character and worth of each person's work. If any person's work which he has built [on this foundation, that is, any outcome of his effort] remains [and survives this test], he will receive a reward. But if any person's work is burned up [by the test], he will suffer the loss [of his reward]; yet he himself will be saved, but only as [one who has barely escaped] through fire.
>
> –1 Corinthians 3:11–15

We must seek the Lord in our "quiet place" of communion and prayer so that we can know that our works have been "birthed" in Him. There was a time in my life as a young Christian when I was involved in a lot of "good works" at the church I was attending. I really believed that the Lord was pleased with me. But one day in my prayer time, Jesus showed me that He loved my heart's desire to please Him but that He wanted **me** more than my **works**. They were "good works," but they were not "God-works." The Lord had other things that He wanted to do *in* and *through* my life. Jesus told me to lay down all of the spiritual activities that I was doing at church and to come and spend more time with Him. I must admit that it was hard at first. As I let go of all my activity, Jesus showed me that I was trying to earn the love and the favor of God by my works. I felt that I had little value in His Kingdom when I wasn't busy, and this was a deep heart-issue that Jesus wanted to confront and change.

We must build on the foundation of Christ which means doing what He wants to do in and through our lives not what *we think* He wants us to do. Works that will not burn up on that "Day" are gold, silver, and precious stones; these are the works that the Spirit "births" in and through us as He "overshadows" us. It is during these times of sweet communion with our Savior that He "downloads" into our hearts His will and His purpose for our lives. This does not happen overnight but week after week, month after month, and year after year as we commune with our King. He will release His desires and His purpose for our lives as we grow spiritually through listening and obeying His voice. As we cultivate this in our lives, we will find that we are truly "living sacrifices" for our King in all that we do. We do not want to stand before the Lord on that great "Day" and see our works burned up. Now is the time to press deeply into the heart of God and to make sure that we are doing His will and not ours.

> There remains therefore a rest for the people of God. For he who has entered His rest has himself also ceased from his works as God did from His.
> –Hebrews 4:9–10 – NKJV

This is the time and the season to enter fully into the rest that God is calling us into. This rest is God's very presence inside of us as we abide in Him, yield to His will, and allow the Spirit to work <u>His</u> works through our lives. We must stop going our own way and listening to our own thoughts, for we know that God's ways and thoughts are so much higher than ours. (See Isaiah 55:8–9.)

Hear what Jesus would speak to your heart:

> *"I have called you to be a 'living sacrifice' for Me not a 'dead' one filled with self-works and the things of this world. I have called you, children; can you hear the cry of My heart in this hour? The time is short, much shorter than you think, before My coming on 'clouds of glory.' You must be ready; you must be prepared for your eternal position and place in Me.*
>
> *"This is a serious word and a serious time that you live in. Let go of all your earthly 'toys' and embrace My plan and purpose*

for your life. I have called you to be a 'living sacrifice,' alive in Me, walking in Me, abiding in Me, and obeying Me in all the things that I would ask you to do.

"To be a 'living sacrifice' you must live and move in Me fully. This is not a 'partial' sacrifice but a sacrifice of your 'whole' life surrendered fully to Me. Your focus must be completely on Me and what I am doing in this hour not on what man is doing or what others are doing around you. All must be laid on My 'altar of sacrifice,' your past, your present, and your future. It is then that you will be set apart for Me...a holy and acceptable sacrifice before Me. I will not accept any sacrifice of your flesh or soulish realm. This would be an unacceptable sacrifice, even as the sacrifice of Cain was not offered according to My will and way. There is only one way, and that is the way of My cross: <u>surrender and obedience to Me—above all!</u> I will accept nothing less, children. It is all or nothing if you desire to come into the fullness that I have for you—your full destiny and calling in Me.

"As My 'living sacrifice' you will rescue the perishing, the dying souls all around you. You must be filled with My Life, My love, and My power in order to accomplish this. My Spirit must have full control over your life. He must rule and reign in your heart and your life fully in order for My power to flow through you unhindered. Every 'rock,' 'stone,' and 'thorn' must be removed from your heart, and you cannot do this in your own strength. (See Mark 4:1–20.) This work of My Spirit will be accomplished deep in your soul as you yield to Him completely. This is what I am asking of you in this hour, and like the 'yes' that came from Mary, I am looking for that 'yes' in your heart this very day.

"Release all your cares, anxieties, and strife, come to My 'altar' this day, and lay your whole life before Me, and I will accept you as My 'living sacrifice'—says your God!"

A Sword Will Enter Your Heart

> And Joseph and His mother marveled at those things which were spoken of Him. Then Simeon blessed them, and said to Mary His mother, "Behold, this Child is destined for the fall and rising of many in Israel, and for a sign which will be spoken against (yes, **a sword will pierce through your own soul also)**, that the thoughts of many hearts may be revealed."
> –Luke 2:33–35, emphasis added

> But Mary treasured all these things, pondering them in her heart.
> –Luke 2:19 – NASB

When glorious words and prophesies were spoken over Jesus' life by the angel Gabriel, Simeon, John the Baptist, Anna in the temple, the shepherds at His birth, and others, Mary treasured all these words in her heart. I don't believe that Mary knew the extent of what she would suffer as she lived her life out before God, but she was determined to do God's will, no matter the cost. When Simeon told Mary that a sword would pierce through her own soul also, she must have thought about this word and pondered on it through the days, weeks, months, and even years ahead. She had already been through some deep suffering, but there would be much more to come. I believe that more than one "sword" pierced Mary's heart throughout her earthly journey.

Think of what Mary must have suffered through the slander and gossip of those who lived in Nazareth where she lived. I'm sure Mary wept many tears and felt this "sword" pierce her heart, but she was strengthened and comforted by the Lord through her ordeals. She had faith and knew without a doubt that she was carrying and would birth the One who was the Savior of the world. This must have been her greatest comfort. Joseph also suffered tremendously, for it's very likely that some must have believed that he was the one who got her pregnant. Even after the birth of Jesus and seeing the miracles, signs, and wonders that followed Him, many Pharisees and others, even His own brothers, did not believe that He was the Messiah. (See Mark 3:22; John 7:3–5, 7:10–13, 7:20; 8:19.) This must have cut deeply into the soul of Mary.

> Mary, Jesus' mother, was standing next to His cross, along with Mary's sister, Mary the wife of Clopas, and Mary Magdalene.
> –John 19:25 – TPT

Mary stood with her Son throughout His life, through all the ups and the downs, all the joys and the sorrows, and all the pain and the misunderstandings. This "sword" that Simeon spoke of was experienced throughout her life, but the deepest cut would come as she stood by the cross and watched her beloved Son anguish in pain and die. As her Son was taking His last breath, she stood next to His cross. She had learned to carry her own cross through all that she had suffered, and now she was able and had the inner strength to stand with her Son as He suffered the agony of the cross. No tongue can tell what Jesus went through on that dark and grievously painful day. It must have been a deep comfort for Jesus to see His mother near His cross, to know that she loved Him and believed that He was the Messiah, the Savior of the world. I believe that when Mary gazed upon her Son on the cross, she remembered the prophecy Simeon spoke to her so many years earlier. What deeper sorrow could Mary feel than watching Jesus suffer and die before her?

> For the word of God is living and active and full of power [making it operative, energizing, and effective]. It is sharper than any two-edged sword, penetrating as far as the division of the soul and spirit [the completeness of a person], and of both joints and marrow [the deepest parts of our nature], exposing and judging the very thoughts and intentions of the heart. And not a creature exists that is concealed from His sight, but all things are open and exposed, and revealed to the eyes of Him with whom we have to give account.
> –Hebrews 4:12–13 – AMP

Many times our scars are not visible to the naked eye, but they are just as real and just as painful. We go through "beatings" when people tear us down emotionally. Sexual abuse and "cutting" words can pierce us and bring us to our knees in brokenness. Betrayal is another sharp "sword" that will cut to the deepest places in our hearts. Divorce, physical sickness, the death of a loved one, losses of all kinds, all of these and more will break us as we walk with Jesus in full surrender and obey His will in all things. God never promised us an easy path, but He promised that He would never leave us nor forsake us. (See Hebrews 13:5.)

This "sword" that the Spirit will use in our lives is a sword of fiery love. It is sharp; it will penetrate deep into our hearts and souls and will show us the motives and intents of our heart. It is a painful sword, but it is one that brings life and freedom to our souls and even our bodies. It is a "living and active" sword, not one that we just learn about or think about in our minds but one that we will *experience* in the depths of our heart. It will bring pain and tears but also great joy and deliverance from a past that tries to keep us bound in pain and misery. This sword will reveal to us the works that we are doing in the flesh and soulish realm, and the Spirit will cut this out of our lives if we let Him.

As we read, meditate, and allow the Word of God to penetrate our hearts, it will be used to "wash" us and to "cut away" everything in our hearts that is not of Him. (See Ephesians 5:26.) When we are "doers of the Word" and not "hearers only," this is when we will experience His powerful sword cleansing and energizing us. (See James 1:22.) The Holy Spirit desires to go into the deepest parts of our heart and to remove every sin and iniquity that may still be keeping us bound. God wants to expose the deep, hidden roots of iniquity in our hearts, not to hurt us but to heal us completely and make us whole.

> After sending them out, the LORD God stationed mighty cherubim to the east of the Garden of Eden. And He placed a flaming sword that flashed back and forth to guard the way to the tree of life.
>
> –Genesis 3:24 – NLT

Because of sin, disobedience, and rebellion, Adam and Eve were driven out of the Garden of Eden, and God stationed His angel with a "flaming sword" that guarded the way to the "tree of life." God made a way, through the sacrifice of His Son, to have eternal life and to enter into His glorious Kingdom. Jesus is the Way, the Truth, and the Life, and there is no other way that leads to salvation; His cross alone brings "Life" to those who are "dead" in their sin. (See John 14:6.) We know that Jesus died on a "tree," an "old wooden cross," and became the "Tree of Life" for all of mankind. Everyone who receives Him will now experience eternal life in Him. Through the blood of Jesus the way into eternal life has been opened, and now we can eat from the "Tree of Life," Jesus, the "Bread from Heaven," and live eternally. (See John 3:35–36.)

God protected Adam and Eve from eating this tree, for He did not want them to live eternally in their sin. (See Genesis 3:22.) As God's flaming sword works deep in our hearts and cuts away sin and iniquity, we will once again be able to enter into His "Garden of Eden," His Promised Land. We will then be able to *fully* enjoy all that the Lord has planned for our lives. Only through the shed blood of Jesus can we come back to the place that Adam and Eve lost because of disobedience and enjoy the abundant life that God has promised us. Now is the time to take back all that the enemy has stolen from us!

The Fellowship of Sufferings

I love Baker's definition of the word **fellowship:** "First, the fact and experience of Christian fellowship only exists because God the Father through Jesus Christ, the Son, and by/in the Spirit has established in grace a relation (a 'new covenant') with humankind. Those who believe the gospel of the resurrection are united in the Spirit through the Son to the Father. The relation leads to the reality of relatedness and thus to an experienced relationship (a 'communion') between man and God. And those who are thus 'in Christ' (as the apostle Paul often states) are in communion not only with Jesus Christ (and the Father) in the Spirit but also with one another. This relatedness, relationship, and communion is fellowship."[iv]

Through the blood of Jesus and the New Covenant, we can now enter "behind the veil," for it has been rent, opened up to all who have truly received Jesus into their hearts and lives. (See Matthew 27:51.) All who are in Christ can now enter into the Holy of Holies and have sweet communion with their Savior. (See Hebrews 10:19-22.) We can now have deepest intimacy and a glorious relationship with Jesus…a love feast in Him. We can now share not only His deepest joys but also His sufferings. If we truly want to <u>know</u> Jesus, we must share in His sufferings as "good soldiers." (See 2 Timothy 2:3.)

In a deep friendship we want to celebrate not only our friends' joys but also their concerns and sorrows. We stand by their side no matter what they are going through, whether it be deepest sorrow or greatest joy. This is how a deep relationship grows in love, trust, and true commitment to those we love. How much more should we long to know the heart of Jesus and all that concerns Him? Jesus wants us to experience the depths of His heart: His love for us and for the lost and also His deepest joys as we follow Him in full commitment to His will. As the Spirit deepens His life in us, we are then more fully conformed into the image of His Son. Pain and suffering "cuts" deep "crevices" into our hearts, and it is then that the Spirit comes and fills the empty places in our hearts with Jesus' fiery love.

> And this, so that I may know Him [experientially, becoming more thoroughly acquainted with Him, understanding the remarkable wonders of His Person more completely] and [in that same way experience] the power of His resurrection [which overflows and is active in believers], and [that I may share] the fellowship of His sufferings, by being continually conformed [inwardly into His likeness even] to His death [dying as He did]; so that I may attain to the resurrection [that will raise me] from the dead.
> –Philippians 3:10–11 – AMP

Mary knew the "fellowship of His sufferings" deeply. She walked with her Son through all the fiery trials of life. She allowed the Spirit to break open her heart so that God's love and grace could pour into the depths of her being. She wanted to know the Lord and His power in order to overcome every "mountain" that stood in her way. She had much joy in her life, but she also suffered great emotional pain and grief.

Even though the Scriptures do not reveal much concerning the childhood of Jesus, I believe they reveal the closeness that Jesus and His mother had. Her love and concern for Him was strong, and I'm sure Jesus shared many of His joys and sorrows with her. But as the Scriptures show us, Jesus' relationship with His heavenly Father was always top priority. We will expound on this in the next section of this book.

If we do not allow our hearts to be broken with Jesus, we will only have a shallow relationship with Him, but if we allow the Spirit to break open our hearts and come to know the "fellowship of sufferings" with Jesus, we will develop a deep and lasting relationship with Him. Not only will we weep with Jesus in His pain, but we will laugh with Him in His joys. As we walk with Jesus and embrace our cross, we will also come to know the "power of His resurrection." If we refuse to embrace our cross and fellowship with Him in His sufferings, we will never know the *fullness* of His resurrection power. If we truly want to *know* Jesus, there is no other way than to pick up our cross daily and follow Him all the way to Calvary, the grave, and then into the power of His resurrection.

> But Jesus answered them by saying, "The hour has come for the Son of Man to be glorified. Truly, truly I say to you, unless a grain of wheat falls into the earth and dies, it remains alone; but if it dies, it bears much fruit. The one who loves his life loses it, and the one who hates his life in this world will keep it to eternal life. If anyone serves Me, he must follow Me; and where I am, there My servant will be also; if anyone serves Me, the Father will honor him."
> –John 12:23–26 – NASB

In order to bear much fruit for our Savior, we must be as a "grain of wheat," be "buried" in the ground, and "die" to all that takes precedence over Jesus. Jesus must be our "first love." This does not mean that we do not love or care for others, but our relationship with Jesus must be our *first* priority. His will for our lives must be placed above our own will and what others desire for our lives. For many people this is too great a price for them to pay, for their hearts have placed people and things before Jesus.

Jesus tells us that if we love our lives we will lose them, but if we hate our lives in this world we will keep them to eternal life. This is a message that many ministers do not preach or teach God's people, and they will be held accountable before the Lord for the "light" Gospel message that they preach. God's people need to hear the *whole* Truth of the Gospel not just partial truths that keep them in their sin and rebellion. We are called to follow Jesus, not man or the ways of the world. Only when we put Jesus *first* and serve Him *above all* will we be honored by the Father when we enter through the "Gates of Heaven."

> If the world hates you, you know that it has hated Me before it hated you. If you were of the world, the world would love you as its own; but because you are not of the world, but I chose you out of the world, because of this the world hates you. Remember the word that I said to you, "A slave is not greater than his master." If they persecuted Me, they will persecute you as well; if they followed My word, they will follow yours also.
> –John 15:18–20

Jesus knew what it was like to be slandered and rejected, and in the same way when we surrender fully to the Father's will, we, too, will be hated by this world. If we have true and deep fellowship with Jesus, we will speak the whole counsel of God's Word, and believe me, many will *not* like it. We will suffer slander, persecution, demonic attacks that will seem relentless, losses, and many fiery trials. When you go downstream with the crowd, you will suffer little, but choose to go upstream and follow the Lord on His path, it is then that you will know much pressure and misunderstandings from those around you, and many will malign your name and speak evil about you. In all of this you will know that you are walking on that "hard path" and going through the "narrow gate" that brings true life. (See Matthew 7:13–14.) We are not here to be praised by others but to please our heavenly Father by speaking Truth no matter the cost. (See Luke 6:26.)

We are not of this world; Jesus chose us to come out of this world system, and because of this we will be hated. This is a promise from Jesus. It is something that we *will* experience. We are His "love slaves," and we are not greater than our Master. They persecuted Jesus, and people will persecute us. Why do we question when we experience hate and rejection in this world? If others follow the Truth of God's Word, they will listen to us and follow us, but if they are going the way of the world, they will come against us and persecute us. This is God's word to us in this hour.

> Now large crowds were going along with Him, and He turned and said to them, "If anyone comes to Me and does not hate his own father, mother, wife, children, brothers, sisters, yes, and even his own life, he cannot be My disciple. Whoever does not carry his own cross and come after Me cannot be My disciple. For which one of you, when he wants to build a tower, does not first sit down and calculate the cost, to see if he has enough to complete it? Otherwise, when he has laid a foundation and is not able to finish, all who are watching it will begin to ridicule him, saying, 'This person began to build, and was not able to finish!' Or what king, when he sets out to meet another king in battle, will not first sit down and consider whether he is strong enough with ten thousand men to face the one coming against him with twenty thousand? Otherwise, while the other is still far away, he sends a delegation and requests terms of peace. So then, none of you can be My disciple who does not give up all his own possessions."
>
> –Luke 14:25–33

Mary placed the will of God for her life above her own will. She counted the cost when she bowed her head and embraced the word of the Lord through the angel Gabriel. Granted, she didn't have much time to think it over, but she loved God and trusted that He knew what was best for her life. She was a true follower of the "Living God." Mary's immediate "yes" to the word of the Lord spoken to her shows us that her heart already belonged to God and that she was willing to go through whatever was necessary to fulfill her destiny.

Have we counted the cost and what it means to truly follow Jesus *all the way*? Have we been "building" up our spiritual lives and following Jesus but now believe that we cannot finish the race because of some fiery trial that has brought us to our knees? The Bible tells us not to be surprised because of the trials that we find ourselves in and look at them as "strange." So why do so many get angry with God and turn back to the things of this world when they are tested in this way? (See 1 Peter 4:12.) These trials come to test and purify us; nothing we go through is in vain.

Are we willing to give up all of our possessions out of love for Jesus and surrender all, no matter what losses we suffer? It's easy to say, "yes" when things are going our way and we are not in a "crucible of suffering," but when God's holy fire is truly ignited in our lives, there is a great struggle in our heart that often comes with many tears. The cross is NEVER easy, and anyone who believes that it is has not truly taken up their cross and followed Jesus all the way to Calvary.

I think of this song written long ago called: **I Have Decided to Follow Jesus**[v] by Sundar Singh:

> I have decided to follow Jesus;
> I have decided to follow Jesus;
> I have decided to follow Jesus;
> No turning back, no turning back.
>
> The world behind me, the cross before me;
> The world behind me, the cross before me;
> The world behind me, the cross before me;
> No turning back, no turning back.
>
> Though none go with me, still I will follow;
> Though none go with me, still I will follow;

Though none go with me, still I will follow;
No turning back, no turning back.

My cross I'll carry, till I see Jesus;
My cross I'll carry, till I see Jesus;
My cross I'll carry, till I see Jesus;
No turning back, no turning back.

Will you decide now to follow Jesus?
Will you decide now to follow Jesus?
Will you decide now to follow Jesus?
No turning back, no turning back.

Remember: "Blessed is the man who endures temptation; for when he has been approved, he will receive the crown of life which the Lord has promised to those who love Him" (James 1:12 – NKJV).

Listen to the voice of Jesus saying:

"Welcome the pain; embrace the difficult path that I have placed you on, for this is the path and the place of transformation. Like Paul, you have chosen what is perfect in My sight, and these 'crosses' in your life are conforming you into the very image of My Son. None of this is wasted.

"Many choose the 'easy road,' the 'wide gate,' but this is not the place of transformation and freedom in My Spirit. (See Matthew 7:13–14.) Out of 'death to self' comes resurrection power. I only anoint what is 'dead'...flesh that has been crucified, a soul that has been renewed in My Word, and a mind transformed into the 'mind of Christ.'

"The 'light' path never accomplishes My full will for your life. It is the hard path that causes you to run to Me...to surrender to Me, and that makes you strong in My Spirit. I am out to make you strong warriors not wimpy whiners. I am calling you to a place of full surrender and obedience to My will. Forever put the easy way out of your life; embrace your cross fully and follow

Me all the way to Mount Calvary...to the tomb and then into My resurrection power.

"Now is the time, now is the season for a full, sacrificial laying down of your life, your will, and your own plans for your life. I am the Lord your God who is crying out to you in this hour to release your life fully to Me so that I can implement all that I have planned for you: your destiny and your calling in Me. You cannot comprehend all that I have for you in this hour, but it will only come forth as you surrender your whole life: your mind, will, and emotions fully to Me. I will come with My fire as you lay your life on My 'altar,' and I will accept your life as a 'living sacrifice,' holy and acceptable to Me.

"So, come close to Me in this hour—closer than you ever have before, and I will transform your life into My fullness, into My glory, and you will know, without a doubt, that you have chosen the right path, the 'narrow path' that I have chosen for your life—says your God."

Who is My Brother, Sister, and Mother?

"The one who has My commandments and keeps them is the one who loves Me; and the one who loves Me will be loved by My Father, and I will love him and will reveal Myself to him." Judas (not Iscariot) said to Him, "Lord, what has happened that You are going to reveal Yourself to us and not to the world?" Jesus answered and said to him, "If anyone loves Me, he will follow My word; and My Father will love him, and We will come to him and make Our dwelling with him."

–John 14:21–23 – NASB

The Scripture above shows us that if we truly love Jesus we will keep His commandments. In keeping His commands and doing what the

Spirit is telling us to do, we will then come to know the deep love of the Father. Jesus will come to us and reveal Himself to us in new and glorious ways. This is the only way that we can show Jesus that we truly love Him: not by the words that we speak or the songs that we sing but by obeying His written Word and *doing* what He tells us to do.

If we truly love Jesus we will follow His Word; we will not only be *hearers* of His Word but *doers* of it. (See James 1:22.) When we walk in obedience to the will of the Father, we will experience the indwelling of God inside of our spirit, soul, and even our bodies. As we continue our walk of obedience and obey the Lord in all things, we will come to know the *fullness* of the Spirit. How glorious it is to know the presence of the "Living God" inside of our earthly "temples!" There is no greater joy in the whole earth than this!

> Then His mother and brothers came to Him, and could not approach Him because of the crowd. And it was told Him by some, who said, "Your mother and Your brothers are standing outside, desiring to see You." But He answered and said to them, "My mother and My brothers are these who hear the word of God and do it."
> –Luke 8:19–21 – NKJV

Here Jesus shows us the importance of obeying God's Word—above all. Jesus put obedience to the will of God above everything else in His life, even above His relationship with His mother and His earthly family members. He loved and respected His mother, sisters, and brothers, but there was nothing higher or more valuable to Him than obeying His heavenly Father.

There will be times in our lives when the Lord will ask us to do something that our family members may not agree with. They may feel that what God has called us to do is too dangerous, or they may have other plans for our lives. They may question why we "love Jesus" <u>more</u> than them. Many, many people, even in the Church, put their families and loved ones before God and His will for their lives. Why do we place such a high value on those who join the military and leave their families to serve and maybe even die for their country but those who surrender all for Jesus and obey Him are called "foolish?"

Who are we going to submit to? If we put our relationship with our loved ones above our relationship with Jesus, we may pull back from doing what God is asking us to do. Jesus made a very strong point here when He told the crowd that His mother and His brothers are those who hear the Word of God and _do_ it. This is the value that Jesus puts on obedience. Nothing less will please our Savior.

> As He was speaking, a woman in the crowd called out, "God bless your mother—the womb from which you came, and the breasts that nursed you!" Jesus replied, "But even more blessed are all who hear the word of God and put it into practice."
> –Luke 11:27–28 – NLT

In the above Scriptures we see that a woman in the crowd wanted to exalt Mary in a way that would put the emphasis on Jesus' mother as the one who carried Jesus in her body and who nursed Him. Instead, Jesus redirected the spotlight to the importance of hearing the Word of God and putting it into practice. Even now many put Mary in a higher position than what God desires. They place her as another "mediator," another avenue to reach God. Mary was blessed, but Jesus said that even more blessed are those who follow and obey Him.

Even back then, thousands of years ago, Jesus showed us that the most important thing in our lives is following Him and His Word. It is not following another person no matter how influential they are. So many in the Church put other people on pedestals and listen to them more than the voice of the Spirit. They take their words as "gospel" and do not even bother going to the Word to see if what they teach or preach is Truth. We must pray, study God's Word, and do only what He tells us to do. Others may try to influence us and to tell us what to do, but we must always go back to our "secret place" and pray to see if this is God's will for our lives. God's people must grow and mature into the "full stature of Christ," and then they will no longer be tossed about by every "wind of doctrine" that they hear. (See Ephesians 4:13–14.)

Jesus loved His mother deeply, but He made it clear to her and to us that nothing is more important than following His Word and applying it to our lives. The Lord was in no way down-playing Mary's role in birthing Him, in being His earthy mother, but His emphasis was on the importance of doing the Father's will. Jesus did only what He saw the Father doing; nothing more, nothing less. (See John 5:19.) For Jesus nothing was higher, nothing was greater than accomplishing what His Father had planned for His life even though it cost Him pain beyond measure and His eventual death on the cross. This was the passion of His life, and He wants this to be our passion also. Mary's passion was to do God's will—above all, so let's follow her example and obey the Lord in all things.

Hear the voice of your Father:

> *"Come near to Me and let go of all distractions. This recent 'blow' is not meant to discourage you but to detach you from your own will and to embrace Mine. It is not meant to destroy you but to release you into the fullness that I have for you. This earthly plane is a place of deep testing, and the testing of your faith will mature you and bring you to the place that I have for you, a place of stability in Me, a place of true faith and trust in Me, no matter your circumstances.*
>
> *"It is not easy to come to this place, for it is a place where all must be laid before Me in complete and total surrender to My will. The flesh and soulish realms die hard, children, and this is only right, for what I have for you is Spirit-born and more glorious than your heart could ever conceive or understand. This place of 'death' brings life eternal into every nerve and every cell in your body. It releases your soul and brings it into what is truly important and valuable on this earthly plane.*
>
> *"It is not head-knowledge but heart-knowledge of who I am and what I desire to work in and through your life. This is not a 'light' work but a deep, internal change that is forming you into My very image. Those who proclaim and teach that it is an 'easy road' have not been through this deep, internal transformation,*

and the works they release bring only surface change. I am after the heart; I am after the deepest recesses of the heart in this hour, and I desire to pull up the deepest roots of iniquity that have bound countless millions of souls. This is a deep work, children, and you are not to take this lightly. I am bringing a bright search light into the depths of your being in order to show you what lies in the depths of your heart. I am the One who will expose these deep, hidden roots, things you cannot see in the natural, that have bound you to this earth's culture and ways. This is a deep, hidden, dark place that you have been fearful of, but I will give you great courage to look at these 'iniquitous patterns' in your life and at last be completely freed from them.

"No more 'surface works,' children. My desire is to birth in you My Spirit's plan and destiny in your life. This work will be completed quickly now, and you will understand what I have been after all along. This is NOT a work of condemnation but a work that will free you to be all that I have created you to be.

"Rejoice in this, children, for what I am about to accomplish in your life will cause you to soar with 'wings as an eagle.' You are called to walk with Me in the High Place of surrender and glory, and this is the place that I am bringing you into now. Rejoice in this and fear not, for truly you will now see Me face-to-face in an intimacy and glory you have not known in the past—says your God!"

Chapter 3
The Divine Turnaround

When everything around you looks dark, can you still believe for a divine turnaround in your life? Or do you believe that things will go from bad to worse? This is the time and the season when God wants us to have faith for the miraculous…to believe that what looks impossible can be turned for our good and for God's glory. In this season when it looks like the enemy has the upper hand, are you believing that the Almighty King of the Universe can reverse the tables and bring the glorious changes in this world that He desires to bring forth?

We are going to see divine reversals in ways that will astound us, and many, even those in the Church who have grown discouraged and turned back to the things and the ways of this world, will now make a U-turn and seek Jesus with their whole heart. They will turn back to the "old ancient paths" of repentance, holiness, and righteousness and find the One that they truly love. (See Jeremiah 6:16.) They will come back to their "first love." (See Revelation 2:4.)

> After the celebration was over they started home to Nazareth, but Jesus stayed behind in Jerusalem. His parents didn't miss Him the first day, for they assumed He was with friends among the other travelers. But when He didn't show up that evening, they started to look for Him among their relatives and friends; and when they couldn't find Him, they went back to Jerusalem to search for Him there. Three days later they finally discovered Him. He was in the Temple, sitting among the teachers of Law, discussing deep questions with them and amazing every-

one with His understanding and answers. His parents didn't know what to think. "Son!" His mother said to Him. "Why have you done this to us? Your father and I have been frantic, searching for you everywhere." "But why did you need to search?" He asked. "Didn't you realize that I would be here at the Temple, in My Father's House?" But they didn't understand what He meant.

–Luke 2:43–50 – The Living Bible

Mary and Joseph had to back track, make a U-turn, and go all the way back to Jerusalem in order to find Jesus, and in the same way those who have wandered far from Jesus will have to turn around and repent in order to "find" Him again. He hasn't moved away from them, but they have drifted back into the world or disobeyed the Lord in some area of their lives. It's like an example I once heard: There was someone in the passenger seat in a car, and they turned and said to the driver: *"Why have you moved so far away from me?"* The driver then said: *"I'm not the one who moved!"* Jesus hasn't moved away from His people or this generation, but many have moved away from Him and have gone their own way, even in the Church.

This is the time and the season when we cannot afford to be spiritually lazy or lax in seeking the Lord and doing His will. We are in a very late hour, and the Lord has revealed to me that the hour is later than we think. Many are still playing with the things of this world and are also involved in ministries that are not "birthed" in the Spirit. We must use our time wisely, for in a very short time we will see dramatic changes in this world, and we must be fully prepared. The turnarounds in our nation and this world are going to come fast and be furious.

When we are young, spiritually, and Jesus begins to move a little ahead of us, we do not always discern His absence immediately, just like Mary and Joseph didn't miss Him the *first* day. There are times when we miss a day of reading the Word or spending time with our Heavenly Father, and it doesn't seem to bother us. But if we continue to miss our daily time with the Lord, we may begin to feel a little "irritable" and wonder why we feel uneasy. We may still be doing good works and not blatantly sinning, but we still feel that there is something "amiss." This is the Lord's love call to come back to the "secret place" and to spend precious time with Him, pouring out our hearts and listening to His sweet voice. We must never put our time spent with Jesus on the "back burner."

Many of God's children have fallen away in this hour because of church closures or their own deep discouragement because of the fiery trials and the darkness that has enveloped our nation and this world. There are some that believe that going to church is not important…that they can seek the Lord on their own or just watch the church service on-line and be blessed. This may be okay for a short season because of various circumstances, but I have found that there is nothing like going to church and being with those of like-faith.

The glory and presence of God in a church setting is glorious. There is no substitute. Some of God's people have established house-churches, and this is great if the Lord has led you in this direction. The most important thing is to be with other Believers so that you can build up each other in the faith and be accountable to those in your "circle."

Jesus would say to those who feel they have "lost" Him the same words that He spoke to Mary and to Joseph: *"But why did you need to search? Didn't you realize that I would be here at the Temple, in My Father's House?"* Mary and Joseph didn't understand how deep the passion in Jesus' heart was in seeking His Father and neither do some of God's children realize that the most important thing in this life is passionately seeking Jesus and listening to His voice. There needs to be a drastic, even "violent," turnaround in our lives if the things of this world are distracting us and are drawing us away from the presence of our God. This divine turnaround is not always comfortable as we will now see in the Song of Solomon.

> I slept, but my heart was awake, when I heard my lover knocking and calling: "Open to me, my treasure, my darling, my dove, my perfect one. My head is drenched with dew, my hair with the dampness of the night." But I responded, "I have taken off my robe. Should I get dressed again? I have washed my feet. Should I get them soiled?" My lover tried to unlatch the door, and my heart thrilled within me. I jumped

up to open the door for my love, and my hands dripped with perfume. My fingers dripped with lovely myrrh as I pulled back the bolt. I opened to my lover, but he was gone! My heart sank. I searched for him but could not find him anywhere. I called to him, but there was no reply. The night watchmen found me as they made their rounds. They beat and bruised me and stripped off my veil, those watchmen on the walls. Make this promise, O women of Jerusalem— If you find my lover, tell him I am weak with love.

–Song of Solomon 5:2–8 – NLT

By night on my bed I sought the one I love; I sought him, but I did not find him. "I will rise now," I said, "and go about the city; in the streets and in the squares I will seek the one I love." I sought him, but I did not find him. The watchmen who go about the city found me; I said, "Have you seen the one I love?" Scarcely had I passed by them, when I found the one I love. I held him and would not let him go.

–Song of Solomon 3:1–4a – NKJV

Many scholars believe that the Shulamite woman represents the bride of Christ and that the bridegroom represents Jesus.[vi] There are many Scriptures in God's Word that confirm that Jesus is the Bridegroom. One day He will marry His bride, and there will be a glorious wedding feast. (See Matthew 9:15; Mark 2:19; Luke 5:34; John 3:29; Isaiah 54:5; Revelation 19:7–9; 2 Corinthians 11:2; Ephesians 5:25–27.)

The Shulamite "maiden" in the above Scriptures loved her "bridegroom" passionately. Even while she slept her heart was awake, and she heard her beloved knocking and calling her to open to him. In the same way Jesus is crying out to His people to open their hearts to Him more fully in this hour and to abandon all to Him, no matter the cost. Jesus is calling His true children into a new place and a new position of authority and power in Him. For many of His children this will require a divine turnaround, and as they make this turn it will catapult them into their destiny and calling.

I believe that Revelation 3:20 is not only for unbelievers but also for the Church in this hour. This Scripture states: *"Behold, I stand at the door and knock. If anyone hears My voice and opens the door, I will come in to him and dine with him, and he with Me."* Jesus is knocking on the hearts "door" of millions in this hour, and many are responding and opening their hearts to Jesus and to His call, their destiny in Him.

Have you heard the Lord knocking on the "door of your heart" and asking you to make a drastic U-turn in your life? Do you hear Jesus asking you to open your heart more fully to Him and to take a step of faith that you have never taken before? It may be that Jesus is asking you to step out of the boat, that place of comfort, and walk on the "water" with Him to unknown places. Perhaps He is asking you to do what you believe is "impossible." This is the time and the season of sudden, divine turnarounds that will take your breath away.

This "knocking" on the door is not only on the hearts of individuals but also on the doors of many churches. Jesus' "hair" is drenched with "dew," for He has been left on the outside of many churches and has not been allowed entrance. His desire is to take the "reins" of the Church and to manifest His power and glory. Many clergy refuse to allow the Spirit of God to enter into their services and release His presence, power, and His glorious gifts. They want *man-made* order in the house of God not *Spirit-controlled* services which may be a little "messy" at times. There is going to be a divine turnaround now that is so powerful, so all-consuming in His Holy Fire, that many will feel uncomfortable and may even try to leave the church service quickly.

Jesus is calling out to His people in this hour to open their hearts to Him more fully so that He can pour a greater portion of His love and presence into them, but this will require a dramatic turnaround for many of His children. The Lord wants to establish His identity more firmly in the hearts and the lives of His people and to show them how **He** sees them, who they **truly** are in Him. This will require some deep and radical surgery in the hearts of those who belong to Jesus. God wants to awaken the hearts of His people fully in this hour, and it will require great change and an unconditional surrender to His will.

The Hebrew meaning of the name Shulamite is: "shalom," meaning peace, completeness, safety, soundness (in body), welfare, health, prosperity, quiet, tranquility, contentment, and friendship.[vii] This shows us how Christ sees His bride: already complete in Him, healed, content in His love, prosperous in every area, and filled with His peace; this is our true identity in Jesus.

The Shulamite woman in these Scriptures did not want to "get dressed" again but wanted to stay comfortable in her "bed," her "secret place" of intimacy and communion with her beloved, but when her beloved touched her heart, she awakened and jumped up to open the door to her lover. As she did she found that her "beloved" was gone. She deeply enjoyed her "secret place" with the one she loved, much like Mary of old who loved to sit at the feet of Jesus, but the Shulamite's "lover" was now calling her to follow him to the "city"…to that place of spiritual activity where she would come to know him more deeply and intimately through suffering. (See Luke 10:38–42.)

As the Shulamite woman pulled back the latch to open the door, her hands dripped with *perfume,* which represents frankincense (prayer) and *myrrh* (a place of suffering).[viii] The Shulamite's "lover" was calling her to come into union with him through suffering even as Jesus is calling us to "fellowship with Him" in His sufferings. As the Shulamite woman searched for her beloved, the night watchmen beat and bruised her in their efforts to stop her, but she would not stop pursuing the one that she passionately loved.

This shows us that when we pick up our cross and follow Jesus into the harvest field, there may be times of deep suffering. There may be a "season" when these "beatings" come from those we love, even church leaders or pastors. These "watchmen" that "wound" us may not be true "shepherds." They may even be "wolves" in sheep's clothing, but God will allow deep times of testing in order to eventually raise us up to a higher spiritual level.

The Shulamite's "lover" was calling her to turn her back on the comforts that she was used to and to follow him into the city…to that place of "activity," and in the same way Jesus is calling us to forsake the things of this world and to follow Him into the harvest field. The maiden's "lover" wanted to lead her into a <u>new</u> place in him. It was not comfortable for her, and it will not be comfortable for us either. She may have feared that she would lose that deep place of intimacy with him, that place she so dearly loved and treasured, but instead it brought her to a place of even *greater* intimacy with him. It will be the same for all who follow Jesus all the way.

Jesus is calling us to the cities, to the nations of this world, and for many of God's children this will be a drastic, divine turnaround for them!

Jesus is calling His bride to come out of her "cave," to turn her back on the comforts of this world, and to follow Him into the harvest field in this hour. She may have to get her feet "dirty," but Jesus will wash her feet and will draw her even closer in the "secret place" of intimacy with Him. The bride may find herself in a place where she does not want to go, but Jesus will deliver her of *all* fear. This Scripture comes to mind from John:21:15–19 (NLT):

> After breakfast Jesus asked Simon Peter, "Simon son of John, do you love me more than these?" "Yes, Lord," Peter replied, "you know I love you." "Then feed my lambs," Jesus told him. Jesus repeated the question: "Simon son of John, do you love me?" "Yes, Lord," Peter said, "you know I love you." "Then take care of my sheep," Jesus said. A third time He asked him, "Simon son of John, do you love me?" Peter was hurt that Jesus asked the question a third time. He said, "Lord, you know everything. You know that I love you." Jesus said, "Then feed my sheep. I tell you the truth, when you were young, you were able to do as you liked; you dressed yourself and went wherever you wanted to go. But when you are old, you will stretch out your hands, and others will dress you and take you where you don't want to go." Jesus said this to let him know by what kind of death he would glorify God. Then Jesus told him, "Follow Me."

Can you hear the Lord speaking these words to you in this hour? Do we love Jesus enough to turn our backs on the comforts of this world, the "conveniences" we have grown used to in our lives? Will we make a complete turnaround, pick up our cross, and follow Jesus even if it involves suffering the "loss of all things?" (See Philippians 3:8.) It is easy to say that we love

Jesus, but if we *truly* love Him we will follow Him down the hard road of self-denial, unconditional surrender, and obedience to His will.

Change is uncomfortable, for it will require a change in the way we think and do things. We will have to *turn our backs* on all that is familiar and follow our King on the hard path that He would lead us on. It is a hard road, but I promise you: It is a glorious path filled with His love and glory. Many are fearful of what God would ask of them and are not willing to pick up their cross daily and follow Jesus. When people are *settled* in a church and have had their feet washed by Jesus, they may find it hard to leave this place of comfort and get their feet "dirty" by going to the highway and byways to bring in the lost and dying. This is why many times God will allow persecution to touch His people, for it will move them out into the world to do His will. (See Acts 8:3–4.) In this divine turnaround we have to let go of what is familiar and follow Jesus no matter where He leads us.

Jesus is calling us to "feed His sheep," and it may lead us to a place we don't want to go. Will we say "Yes" to Jesus no matter where this divine turnaround in our lives would lead us? It is not only a place of suffering and denial but a place of great glory and power…a place of intimacy with Jesus that will take our breath away. In this divine turnaround we will experience both suffering and glory, but it will be worth it when we stand before Jesus on Judgment Day, hear His words of commendation, and are honored in the "Courts of Heaven."

In this divine turnaround Jesus is about to "unlatch" the "doors" in the hearts of millions of people, and they will thrill at the glorious touch of Jesus. They will "jump up" as this Shulamite woman did and open to Jesus, but they may find themselves in a wilderness…a place of preparation where they will seek Him with their whole heart. In this turnaround they will repent and will turn away from the things of this world, for this one touch from Jesus will impassion them to seek Him with everything that is within them. They will be "weak with love" as they run to those who can tell them where they can find their Beloved. When they find Jesus in His fullness, they will never let Him go, and they will go where He wants them to go and will say what He wants them to say. Their whole life will be consumed with doing the Father's will, and they will be willing to lay down their very lives for Him. Now this is what you call a divine turnaround!

I believe that the dream that God gave me that is detailed below was not only for me but for those who have allowed the Spirit of God to purify them deeply these past years and who have gone through fiery trials and deep sorrows. The Lord wants you to know that your days of trial and of suffering are over and that you will now walk in a High Place of glory with Him that will overwhelm you! You have entered into the *next* glory, and now you will have *faith for the miraculous!* (See 2 Corinthians 3:18.)

In this dream I was driving my car down a road, and someone said that I did something illegal. I didn't think that I had, and when I looked to the "left" across the road, I saw that a car was pulled over by a traffic cop. I knew that I wasn't guilty of disobeying any traffic laws, so I kept on driving. As I looked to the right, I saw Betty White walking straight ahead on the "right" side of the road. I drove past her, made a U-turn, and continued driving.

I didn't think much of the dream, but I thought about the name *Betty White* and believed that God was showing me that *white* stands for purity.[ix] However, there was much more to the dream than I realized. A couple of days after having this dream, I was driving in my car with my son, and I saw a license plate in front of me with the name *Betty White* on it.

I burst out laughing and shared with my son the dream I had a few nights before. Seeing Betty White's name on a license plate right after this dream was near impossible so I knew that the Spirit of God wanted to speak to me about it.

First of all, the Lord had me look up the name Betty, and I found that the Hebrew meaning of Betty (Elizabeth) is: "*from Elisheba, meaning either **oath of God**, or God is satisfaction. Also a diminutive of Bethia (daughter or **worshipper of God**), and of Bethany, a New Testament village near Jerusalem.*"[x]

I saw that the name Elizabeth and Betty had the *same* Hebrew meaning. As I prayed about this the Spirit showed me that those who are walking in the words that *Elizabeth* spoke to Mary in Luke 1:45 (ESV): *"And blessed is she who believed that there would be a fulfillment of what was spoken to her from the Lord"* will now experience a glorious, divine turnaround. Jesus showed me that those who have believed His words to them these past years without seeing *immediate* results in the natural, as Mary did, were now "white," purified and sanctified in Him.

This company of true Believer's would now make a U-turn, a 180-degree turn, and see the fulfillment of all that God has promised them! They have stood on His Word, and they will now shout for joy as God brings them into the fullness that He has for them. The Lord's true worshippers will receive a reward from Jesus that will overwhelm them! This has been God's promise, His oath to them, and they will know complete satisfaction as they see with their eyes the *fulfillment* of what God has spoken to them. They will know that all of their spiritual battles and fiery trials have not been in vain.

As I meditated on this dream, the Holy Spirit showed me that the woman who was stopped and pulled over on the "left side" of the street represents those who have *not* believed His promises and have actually come against His true Believer's. They are being "arrested" and will no longer hinder this next move of God. Many have tried to stop this next glorious move of the Spirit by agreeing with the "adversary" and doing his dark works, but this will no longer be allowed in this season of glory.

It is time for those who have believed God's words to them to make this U-turn and to come into the glorious new future that He has prepared for them. This is the season when His glory will come forth in the lives of those who have stood firm in Truth. They have come through great adversity and have overcome much persecution and the torments of the adversary. This is the day and hour to walk with Him, the Living Christ, and to take hold of the new adventure that He has planned for your life. It is not too late; it is only the beginning of your "glory walk" in Jesus!

I rejoiced in this dream from the Lord, personally, for I knew without a doubt that the theme of this book from Luke 1:45 was truly birthed in the Spirit. The prophecy that God gave me below was not only for me but for all who have believed that His promises to them would come to pass.

God is calling all of us to make a drastic U-turn, to come out of any and all dry, dead, religious rituals, to walk with Him, and to take hold of the new adventure that He has planned for us. There are new "mantles" and new assignments waiting for us to receive from Heaven, and we must delay no longer! This is the time for a divine turnaround that will take your breath away!

Hear Jesus speak this word to you:

> "Great change is coming, child; that's why you made the U-turn...a complete turnaround. You have been cleansed and purified in My Son, and nothing, no one, will stop you from moving forward in My Spirit. In this U-turn I have new things for your life. I have 'suddenlies' and an adventure in Me that will cause your heart to explode in joy and excitement.
>
> "The past is gone, and new things have now arrived. Embrace them; know that they are for you and not for someone else. This U-turn will cause you to forget all the things you have suffered in the past in light of all the glorious things you will now enjoy. It is time to feast. It is time for you to walk in the full freedom that I have prepared for you. All the 'stale' and 'mundane' things of the past are now forever gone. You have a 'sunny' future filled with the Light of My Glory!
>
> "You have come far, spiritually, farther than you realize, and I want you to take a deep, spiritual breath now and receive this reviving love and renewal of spirit, soul, and body that I am releasing to you right now. No more darkness; no more depression, and I say to you even now: '**The old is gone and the new has come; now walk in it! Walk in the new and glorious things that I have for you!**' This is the next step in your journey in Me, and you will now know 'fullness of joy.' The days of misery are behind you. You have made the U-turn, and now you will see what I have planned for you all along.
>
> "You have reached the 'pinnacle of glory' in Me—now begin to soar with Me to new places and take new territories. They are glorious; they are grand, and now you will rejoice in the inheritance I have given you. Souls, souls, souls will now come into My Kingdom. This is your inheritance in Me. You will now 'reap' precious souls for Me, for you have 'sown' many tears. Nothing has been in vain—says your God!"

Discerning the Time

How we need to pray for greater discernment in this hour! At times I have prayed for the discernment of Nehemiah (see Nehemiah 6:10–14), and I believe that God delights in answering this prayer. So many are making their own plans for the future and are running to conferences so that they might *hear a word* from the Lord concerning their future. This is the hour when we need to hear *directly* from Heaven concerning our lives, our nation, and the nations of this world. The Holy Spirit wants to speak a "now" word to us so that we can prepare our hearts and our lives to move out with Him quickly and to do the Father's will.

So much is happening in our nation and this world, but millions do not see God's hand in these world events. They do not see that we are moving quickly to the end of days as we have known them. Many are not prepared, and many cannot discern that there is going to be a "tailspin" of not only catastrophic events but also a world-wide awakening from the Lord. They continue to live their lives as if nothing will change even though in the past years there have been many "disturbing" events taking place all around us.

> Then Jesus turned to the crowd and said, "When you see clouds beginning to form in the west, you say, 'Here comes a shower.' And you are right. When the south wind blows, you say, 'Today will be a scorcher.' And it is. You fools! You know how to interpret the weather signs of the earth and sky, but you don't know how to interpret the present times.
> –Luke 12:54–56 – NLT

Much is being "uncovered" in our nation and this world in churches, governments, educational systems, and the health industry including child sex trafficking, abusive leaders, corrupt pastors, and false prophets. Praise God that many are seeing the evil and the darkness exposed in this "uncovering" and are crying out to the Lord to have mercy on them, their families, and the nations. God has been the One exposing all of the darkness and the hypocrisy that we are seeing in order to awaken many souls to truth and repentance.

Those who are in tune with the Spirit and are spending time with Jesus in their "prayer closet" know that we are entering a time where nothing will remain the same. But there will be no fear, for they know that the Lord is in full control. God's throne is established in the heavens, and His Kingdom rules over all. (See Psalm 103:19.) Those who have great discernment from the Spirit have prepared their hearts and their lives, and they will *not* be shaken. They have built their "house" on the solid rock of Christ and His Words, and they will not be shaken when the "floods" come and this world experiences God's judgments. (See Matthew 7:24–27.) Their ears are unstopped, and their eyes can see what the King of Glory is doing.

Millions are waking up because the Lord is exposing and uncovering much evil in our nation and this world, but many are still asleep, even in the Church, for they do not believe that Jesus is coming soon. Many are not ready and are still doing their own will because they are not surrendered to the Lord fully. They believe that they are pleasing the Lord, but in this divine turnaround I believe many more will be awakened out of their spiritual slumber. If people truly believed that the coming of the Lord is imminent, they would be living a different life-style and seeking Him passionately with their whole heart.

There is a flood coming, and it is coming quickly. God's true children have prepared their hearts and their lives and are safe in Jesus, the "Ark of Safety." This is the time to enter fully into Christ: to abide in Him and to allow Him to abide in you. (See John 15: 4–5.) It is not time to entertain ourselves with the things of this world or even to be entertained in the church. This is a serious time, and we are to be spiritually "sober." (See 1 Peter 1:13; Matthew 24:42.)

> When God spoke from Mount Sinai His voice shook the earth, but now He makes another promise: "Once again I will shake not only the earth but the heavens also." This means that all of creation will be shaken and removed, so that only unshakable things will remain. Since we are receiving a Kingdom that is unshakable, let us be thankful

> and please God by worshiping Him with holy fear and awe. For our God is a devouring fire.
>
> –Hebrews 12:26-29

Has your life been "shaken" lately through all of the upheavals we are going through in this hour? Are you blaming the enemy for all that looks out of control and for everything that is happening in your life? God is the One who is doing the shaking in our lives because He wants to *shake* the world, everything that is not of Him, out of us so that we can be more fully prepared for what is coming. The Lord is calling us up to higher ground, to see things from His perspective and not from our own understanding.

I remember years ago I was under demonic attack through a woman at my work place. I had to leave the department and go to the chapel. I prayed and paced back and forth, and then the Spirit of the Lord spoke to me and said: *"Can you see Me in this?"* God wanted me to see that the warfare I was going through was for my good, to show me my deep heart of fear and anger and also to learn to "fight the good fight of faith." (See 1 Timothy 6:12.) The Lord was strengthening me spiritually, but at the time I didn't discern or see His hand in what was happening. Jesus wanted to burn up in me all that was not of Him, for truly He is a consuming fire. Our God is holy, and His Word tells us to be holy as He is holy. (See 1 Peter 1:16.)

This "shaking" has begun in our nation and in this world, and we will see many things that we thought were strong and invincible now fall to the ground. Evil dictators will be dealt with swiftly and powerfully as God's mighty hand of judgment is released. We will see the Lord's divine turnarounds in "seemingly" impossible situations, and many will fall to their knees and cry out to the Living God! Only *unshakable* things will remain. I believe because of the force of this shaking the *fear of God* is going to return to the Church and then to millions in all the nations of this earth. When it's all done and finished, only what is of God will remain because of this "violent" shaking. In light of what we are seeing in this hour, we must be watchful and ready, for the Son of Man will come when least expected. (See Luke 12:40.) Let's pray that we are fully prepared for what lies ahead.

> How powerful is His mighty arm! How He scatters the proud and haughty ones! He has torn princes from their thrones and exalted the lowly. He has satisfied the hungry hearts and sent the rich away with empty hands.
> –Luke 1:51–53 – TLB

Mary had deep discernment, for she could see with her spiritual eyes what the Lord was accomplishing in her generation. Even though she lived in a time of great darkness and upheaval in the natural, she looked beyond what she saw and knew that God was in full control. She could see into the future and knew that the Lord would "scatter the proud" and tear down evil princes from their thrones. She saw divine reversals and how God would satisfy the spiritually hungry and send the rich away empty. She was prepared beforehand for the glorious visitation that she had with the angel Gabriel. She truly was a woman of discernment who had her heart focused on God and what He was doing in her generation.

> When He approached Jerusalem, He saw the city and wept over it, saying, "If you had known on this day, even you, the conditions for peace! But now they have been hidden from your eyes. For the days will come upon you when your enemies will put up a barricade against you, and surround you and hem you in on every side, and they will level you to the ground, and throw down your children within you, and they will not leave in you one stone upon another, because **you did not recognize the time of your visitation.**
> –Luke 19:41–44 – NASB, emphasis added

When Jesus came the first time, many did not recognize the time of their visitation, and I believe it is the same in this very hour. Millions have shut their ears to the words that the Spirit is speaking through His true prophets. They have shut their ears and their hearts; they no longer listen but continue to live their own lives and to go their own way. Even millions that attend church no longer believe in His soon coming. They say: *"What happened to the promise that Jesus is coming again? From before* the times of our ancestors, everything has remained the same since the world was first created." (See 2 Peter 3:4.)

This world is unaware that there is a major "flood of judgment" coming and a down-pouring of the Spirit that will usher in countless millions into His Kingdom. As it was in the days of Noah so it will be at the coming of the Son of Man. *"For in the days before the flood, people were eating and drinking, marrying and giving in marriage, up to the day Noah entered the ark; and they knew nothing about what would happen until the flood came and took them all away. That is how it will be at the coming of the Son of Man"* (Matthew 24:38–39 – NIV).

I believe that Jesus is weeping over this generation because of the "spiritual blindness" that has kept millions from seeing what the Spirit of God is doing. We see that even in the Church many have fallen asleep, spiritually, and do not have eyes to see or ears to hear what God is doing and saying to this very generation. Jesus wants us to discern what He is doing and to recognize that He is about to visit us in ways that will astound us as well as bring judgment and deep terror to those who refuse to repent.

Thank God that in His mercy and love He is sending a 3rd Great Awakening that will bring in more than a billion-soul harvest. I believe this with my whole heart, and in some areas in our nation and this world, this has already begun. God doesn't want this hidden from anyone's eyes, but because of stubbornness and willful ignorance many are spiritually blinded. We need to pray earnestly that blinded eyes will be opened and hardened hearts softened.

Without deep discernment from the Holy Spirit, we will not have faith to walk in the miraculous. If we can't hear what the Spirit is speaking to us and if our eyes are spiritually dull, how can we have the faith that we need to walk on His path of spiritual activity? If we are spiritually blind we will walk in our own thoughts and ways or follow others, and it will be as Jesus said about the Pharisees in Matthew 15:14b (NLT): *"They are blind guides leading the blind, and if one blind person guides another, they will both fall into a ditch."*

In Matthew chapter 24 Jesus tells his disciples what signs will occur before He returns at the end of the age. Jesus told them that there would be: deceivers, wars, rumors of war, famines, earthquakes, persecutions, martyrs, apostasies, betrayals, and false prophets. The love of most people will grow cold, and great deception through false signs and wonders will come forth from the enemy. We have seen all of these things in this hour, but we have yet to see the Gospel preached throughout the *whole* earth. I believe this will come forth quickly now. Jesus tells us that when we see *all* of these things happening, we can know that it (the end) is near, even at the door. Jesus goes on to say to keep "watch" for we do not know on what day He will return. We do not know what day, but we sure know from all that is happening in this hour that this is the generation that will experience the last great outpouring of the Spirit and the judgments of God on this earth.

> For the time is coming when they will no longer listen and respond to the healing words of truth because they will become selfish and proud. They will seek out teachers with soothing words that line up with their desires, saying just what they want to hear. They will close their ears to the truth and believe nothing but fables and myths. So be alert to all these things and overcome every form of evil.
> –2 Timothy 4:3–5a – TPT

Because wickedness has abounded many, even in the Church, live selfish and prideful lives. They no longer pray or seek the direction of the Lord for their lives. They no longer listen to Truth, the whole truth of the Gospel, but desire only a "light," "feel good" message that will "tickle their ears." They desire to hear soothing words that line up with their own desires, not God's! If you try to tell them God's truth about their condition, they will come against you in fierce anger and attack you. They would rather hear the lies of the enemy about how "good" they are; they refuse to repent of their rebellious ways. God help us to be alert in all that is happening around us, for we do not want to be caught in a "web of deception" as the world is!

> Be dressed ready for service and keep your lamps burning.
> –Luke 12:35 – NIV

We are to be dressed in the "robe" of righteousness that Jesus provided for us through His shed blood…dressed with His good works, not ours! Jesus is telling us to be filled with His burning love and with the power of the Holy Spirit. The Church of Jesus needs to be fully awakened and found doing the will of the Father, adorned with the beauty of Christ, and shining for Him so that this dark world can see and come to know Jesus and His great salvation. Only then will the Church experience this great, divine turnaround that He has planned for her.

> Having your conduct honorable among the Gentiles, that when they speak against you as evildoers, they may, by your good works which they observe, glorify God in the day of visitation.
>
> –1 Peter 2:12 – NKJV

God is calling us to be His "light" in this dark world and to walk in the works that He has planned for us. As we walk in holiness and live an uncompromised lifestyle, the ungodly will see our good works, and many will turn from their wicked ways. I believe we are in the day of the Lord's visitation. We can see this because of all the upheaval in this world and the increase of the "birth pangs" all around us! (See Matthew 24:6–8.) Many people who are not even close to Jesus see that this world is being shaken to its core, and they are trembling because of the great changes that are occurring in the whole earth. They know that something is about to explode, and many want to know where they can find safety and rest for their souls.

God, grant your Church *eyes to see* what You are doing in this hour and *ears to hear* the voice of Your Spirit clearly. Grant us the discernment that we need so that we can lead others into Your glorious Kingdom.

Listen to the Lord's heart:

> *"Can you discern the time and the season you are in? Can you look around and see My Spirit moving in your nation and this world even though so much of it looks catastrophic and dark?*
>
> *"My children, I want to increase your faith in this hour, increase My presence in you, and lift you to a higher plane of*

*glory. Your focus must be on Me alone. See Me in everything and know that I alone will **turn the table** on the enemy with My right arm of victory.*

"I have seen your tears and the deep 'well of water' in your soul that is rising and spilling over in your life. Your tears will be as a 'river' as you weep with Me over the destruction of many souls in this hour. You will know My heart and that My desire is not to see any soul perish. My heart is a heart of deepest love, deeper than any ocean and wider than the eternal heavens, but My judgments must come forth now. I have waited and waited, and My Spirit has called and warned and drawn many, but few have responded whole-heartedly to My heart's cry!

"Children, the hour is later than you think. Discern the time and know that this is your last visitation. This is My last call to this wayward world. Know the time of your visitation, for it is not one year from now or even one month from now. It is NOW!

"Can you hear the blast of My trumpet sounding out an alarm to repent and to come back to My heart? Can you hear the cries of the remnant, My faithful children, calling to you, speaking of My love and forgiveness, and telling you to turn from your wicked ways and from the dark ways of this world?

*"There is not much time, and as I have spoken before: 'These are My last warnings, not only to the lost but to those in My Church who are not truly surrendered to Me and My will for their lives.' Many churches will empty now, but they will again be filled with hungry, seeking souls...repentant souls who will weep before Me for their lukewarmness and disobedience. These souls will now take 'seats of honor' in My presence, and many religious 'Pharisees' will step down from their positions and be left behind. Kings and princes, leaders and generals who have lifted themselves up and placed themselves in high positions **apart from Me** will now be humbled in My presence, and some will repent in 'dust and ashes.'*

"I will now raise up the lowly, the forgotten ones, those who have 'hidden' themselves in Me and who have not looked for help

from man but from Me alone. These are the ones that I will now raise up to a High Place of power and of authority. This divine turnaround has arrived. See this, My children, and know that as you see this happening in greater frequency that I am standing at the door and ready to come at a moment's notice—says your God!"

For I consider that the sufferings of this present time are not worthy to be compared with the glory that is to be revealed to us. For the eagerly awaiting creation waits for the revealing of the sons and daughters of God. For the creation was subjected to futility, not willingly, but because of Him who subjected it, in hope that the creation itself also will be set free from its slavery to corruption into the freedom of the glory of the children of God.

–Romans 8:18–21 – NASB

The Great Divide

The Holy Spirit is preparing a bride for Jesus, and a bold "line of division" has already been drawn before the people of God. Those who have stepped over this line into full commitment to the Father's will are even now shining as bright "torches" on the earth. They are dressed in beautiful white garments, and Jesus is removing every last spot and wrinkle from them and making them "white as snow." (See Isaiah 1:18; Psalm 51:7.)

There are many who are making excuses for not going "all the way" with Jesus. They want all the "benefits" of being a "Christian," but they do not love Jesus deeply. The things of this world have captured their hearts, even as Lot's wife turned back to look at what she left behind and was turned into a pillar of salt. (See Genesis 19:26.) The double-minded and compromised soul will never experience the great turnaround and the glorious destiny that God has for them. They make light of being called to the "wedding feast" that the Father has prepared for His Son. They deem the things of this world more important than their eternal souls and their inheritance in Christ. They are as Esau who sold his birthright for a bowl of lentil stew. (See Genesis 25:29–34.)

The things of this world have a "stranglehold" on many, not only on those who are in the world but also on many in the Church, for they do not truly believe that God will take care of all their needs if they abandon all to Jesus. They love this present world and will not let go of their own will and desires. (See 2 Timothy 4:10.) God loves these wayward souls and is calling them daily to let go of the things of this world and come to Him so that He can free them from the chains that tie them to this world. Jesus says that those who refuse to respond to His glorious invitation are not worthy and will in no way enter into His "Banquet Hall." The dividing line has already been drawn, and only those who have stepped over it and have counted the cost will enter into the fullness that He has prepared for their lives.

> And Jesus answered and spoke to them again by parables and said: "The kingdom of heaven is like a certain king who arranged a marriage for his son, and sent out his servants to call those who were invited to the wedding; and they were not willing to come. Again, he sent out other servants, saying, 'Tell those who are invited, "See, I have prepared my dinner; my oxen and fatted cattle are killed, and all things are ready. Come to the wedding."' But they made light of it and went their ways, one to his own farm, another to his business. And the rest seized his servants, treated them spitefully, and killed them. But when the king heard about it, he was furious. And he sent out his armies, destroyed those murderers, and burned up their city. Then he said to his servants, 'The wedding is ready, but those who were invited were not worthy. Therefore go into the highways, and as many as you find, invite to the wedding.' So those servants went out into the highways and gathered together all whom they found, both bad and good. And the wedding hall was filled with guests."
>
> –Matthew 22:1–10 – NKJV

> I came to send fire on the earth, and how I wish it were already kindled! But I have a baptism to be baptized with, and how distressed I am till it is accomplished! Do you suppose that I came to give peace on earth? I tell you, not at all, but rather division. For from now on five in one house will be divided: three against two, and two against three. Father will be divided against son and son against father, mother against daughter and daughter against mother, mother-in-law against her daughter-in-law and daughter-in-law against her mother-in-law.
>
> –Luke 12:49–53

> I baptize you with water for repentance. But after me comes one who is more powerful than I, whose sandals I am not worthy to carry. He will baptize you with the Holy Spirit and fire. His winnowing fork is in His hand, and He will clear His threshing floor, gathering His wheat into the barn and burning up the chaff with unquenchable fire.
>
> –Matthew 3:11–12 – NIV

God's true children have experienced a "baptism of fire," and God is ready to bring them into a glorious U-turn, an explosion of glory in their lives that will overwhelm them! Those who have embraced their cross daily and who are following Jesus will now experience faith to walk into a place they have never walked or known before. It is a place of expansion and power such as they have never experienced in the past. They have not followed Jesus for the blessings He would give them, but out of passionate love they have served their King in obscure places, unknown by this world and the Church. This fire inside their souls and even their bodies has burned up all that is not like Jesus; their motives and their desires have been deeply purified. God can now trust them with greater gifts and a greater anointing.

Jesus is about to send a "fire of judgment" and a "fire of glory" to this earth, and He will separate the holy from the profane. I believe that this generation will experience this great fire, and there will be a greater separation between those who truly love Jesus and those who are just "playing" church. The deep hearts of men are now going to be exposed in a greater way, even what is hidden in the "core" of man's being. All hypocrisy and half-hearted commitments to the Lord will now be exposed. All of the "chaff" in our lives will be burned up in His Holy Fire. Every one of our hearts will experience a fire "seven times hotter" than what we have known in the past, but this is not to be feared by those who have surrendered all to Jesus.

In this "great divide" thousands of Christians in other countries have already experienced great persecution in their families. They have been beaten and thrown out of their homes, and some have even been murdered! In our nation not many have experienced this depth of persecution but have experienced it in a milder yet still painful way. Some have been rejected and excluded from the deep love of their families and have suffered intense demonic warfare, but this, at times, is the cost for giving your all to Jesus. It is a "light affliction" compared to the glory we will know in Jesus; so let's praise our God and know that He alone will never leave us nor forsake us. (See 2 Corinthians 4:17.)

> But when the Son of Man comes in His glory, and all the angels with Him, then He will sit on His glorious throne. And all the nations will be gathered before Him; and He will separate them from one another, just as the shepherd separates the sheep from the goats; and He will put the sheep on His right, but the goats on the left.
> –Matthew 25:31–33 – NASB

When the last great Judgment comes, we will see that even the nations will experience this "great divide." I believe that even now we will see the light and the glory of God resting on cities and nations that have once been clouded with darkness. They will, in this very season, experience a great Light, the Light of the Living Savior. Nations will be judged for either accepting or rejecting the glorious revelation of Jesus in these final hours. An example of this would be North and South Korea. Right now North Korea is experiencing demonic darkness: bondage, persecution, and starvation, but South Korea is experiencing great Light: economic freedom, civil liberty, and freedom of religion. There are nations destined for glory and other nations destined for God's judgment if they continue to refuse His mercy and grace. (See Psalm 2:1–12.)

This is the day and the hour when God will deal with corrupt leaders and will tear down evil empires that have stood strong for many years. I believe that the Lord will release His true children who are trapped in many dark nations, and some of these areas will be flooded with the Light of Jesus in the days ahead. Let's continue to pray for God's persecuted children and for the freedom that they long to experience.

Jesus says:

> *"America shall be saved! This will come about because of My great mercy, long-suffering, and goodness toward My people. Because My remnant has stood firm in faith through much persecution you will now see My hand of mercy and grace descend upon millions of souls freeing them from their captivity.*
>
> *"I have called America and other nations to stand firm in this dark hour so that I might accomplish what man says is impossible. Many think and believe that it is impossible to turn this nation around. They believe that this is the end and that they are already in the 7-year tribulation, but this is not true. I say to you this day:* **'You are on the "outskirts" of My final judgments. It is near, but these final judgments have not come forth yet.'** *This has been a time of testing and a time of separation between the tares and the wheat, not only of individual people but also between 'sheep' and 'goat' nations. (See Matthew 25:31–33.) I have drawn the line, and many are beginning to step over the line and are coming out of darkness and deception. Still, millions upon millions are set on doing their own will and practicing their evil ways.*
>
> *"I am calling My true prophets, teachers, evangelists, pastors, and apostles to speak the whole Truth of the Gospel, the true Gospel, and to preach repentance and full submission to My will in this hour. Many will respond to your message, for they are*

desperate and hungry for Truth, not man's idea of truth but **My Gospel Truth:** *the full Truth as written in My Word. Many souls will come up and out of their 'graves' as you obey Me and minister to these desperate souls the truths written in My Word. Only **full** Truth will I anoint in this hour, and the anointing will break off of their lives the 'yoke' that satan has placed on them. Only My 'living and active' Word can set these 'slumbering' souls free.*

"I have called you, My true and faithful servants, to speak the whole Truth to these captive ones. I will anoint your lips as you speak the full Truth of My Word, and I will give you great boldness in this hour. I will bring My Truth to the forefront now, and you will know the power of My Spirit in a measure you have never experienced before.

"You cannot fathom what I have in store for My faithful warriors in this hour—the strength, power, anointing, love, and glory that I have reserved for My faithful remnant. Now you will see it, My set apart ones, in a wave of glory that will consume your whole life with My fire and My glory. Now you will be lifted up on My wave of glory high above all the dark, distressing clouds of judgment that you will see happening on the earth. I will lift you up, and you will know that you were created 'for such a time as this' to walk with Me in full power... to walk with Me in the miraculous realm that I have foreordained you to walk in.

"Embrace these truths and move forward into your glorious future—says your God!"

There are many "pretenders" that go to church, but they want nothing to do with walking in the true power of the Living Christ. They deny His power to heal and to deliver His children; they do not believe the Truth that the gifts of the Spirit are for God's people in this hour, and they relentlessly persecute those who believe in these gifts. They call the power of God the works of satan, and all those who are in a "living" relationship with Jesus they call deceivers. They do not believe that you can hear the voice of Jesus, and they walk as the Pharisees of old: pretenders and self-righteous hypocrites who will one day have to give account for leading many souls away from the Lord and keeping them "trapped" in their sin and their iniquity because of their false teachings and lies. These false teachers and pastors will now experience this "great divide" as God exposes their sin and brings them down from their position of "false" authority.

> They may pretend to have a respect for God, but in reality they want nothing to do with God's power. Stay away from people like these!
>
> –2 Timothy 3:5 – TPT

> Then the kingdom of heaven will be comparable to ten virgins, who took their lamps and went out to meet the groom. Five of them were foolish, and five were prudent. For when the foolish took their lamps, they did not take extra oil with them; but the prudent ones took oil in flasks with their lamps. Now while the groom was delaying, they all became drowsy and began to sleep. But at midnight there finally was a shout: "Behold, the groom! Come out to meet him." Then all those virgins got up and trimmed their lamps. But the foolish virgins said to the prudent ones, "Give us some of your oil, because our lamps are going out." However, the prudent ones answered, "No, there most certainly would not be enough for us and you too; go instead to the merchants and buy some for yourselves." But while they were on their way to buy the oil, the groom came, and those who were ready went in with him to the wedding feast; and the door was shut. Yet later, the other virgins also came, saying, "Lord, lord, open up for us." But he answered, "Truly I say to you, I do not know you." Be on the alert then, because you do not know the day nor the hour.
>
> –Matthew 25:1–13 – NASB

In this separation and exposure God is separating the 5 foolish virgins from the 5 wise ones who have kept their lamps burning with His Holy Presence inside of them. This is the season that the Lord desires to overflow inside of us and to touch those around us. He is calling us to a passionate "love feast" that will satisfy our hearts completely. Those who have grown spiritually "drowsy" and indifferent to His cries will be left outside and will not enjoy the wedding feast that Jesus has prepared for His true children who have stayed close to Him, obeyed Him, and loved Him passionately. Lukewarm hearts will not enjoy the *full* love and joy of Jesus, and it will be too late for them if they continue to ignore the cries of the Spirit to repent and to draw close to Jesus in this very hour.

Jesus has been crying out to many hearts in this hour and "beseeching" them to let go of the things of this world and to surrender all to Him, but many have refused His love call. What sorrow will fill their hearts when they realize that it is too late for them. The "midnight hour" is fast approaching, and only those that Jesus truly "knows" will enter into this glorious feast that He has prepared for those who love Him. I pray that everyone who reads these words would fully awaken to the love of Jesus and be as those 5 wise virgins who kept their "lamps" filled with oil, the oil of the Holy Spirit and the love of Jesus.

The Spirit of God says:

> *"My 'sword of division' has come, and I am dividing the holy from the profane, the hypocrite from the true Believer, and the sheep from the goat nations. All will see and know that My 'fiery sword' of judgment is accomplishing this powerful work of separation.*
>
> *"This is the time when you will hear great cries of repentance as millions upon millions of souls will* **step over the line** *and consecrate their lives completely and unreservedly to Me. Never has there been a time like the one you are in now. Great cries, great tears, and then great joy will ascend to My throne, and I will respond by releasing millions of captives that the enemy has bound for so long.*

"Discern the time, children, and step over into the fullness that I have for you. Now is the time, not tomorrow, not next month or next year, but NOW! Tomorrow will be too late. Do not be as the 5 foolish virgins who procrastinated and did not keep their 'lamps' filled with My presence. This 'midnight hour' is fast approaching, and only those who have been readied and prepared for My coming will enter in. This is the time to focus and to move with My Spirit courageously and to speak boldly the whole counsel of God.

"I am calling My true warriors to rise up and to call out to those around them, to all I would send them to, to repent and to let go of their 'dead works' and to step over that 'line' that I have drawn before them. There must be a total surrender of their will and a total obedience to all that I ask of them. To all that refuse to surrender, I say: **'You will be left behind to do your own works and will not ride My "High Wave of Glory" in this hour. You will be powerless, and the anointing you once walked in will lift.'** *Remember the life of Saul! I am calling you to full abandonment, children. Move on into the fullness I have for you and enter through the 'narrow gate,' for as you do all the 'baggage' in your life will be left behind.*

"Many see Me as a God that blesses unconditionally no matter how they walk out their lives. They see no requirement, spiritually, for their lives. They say: **'Jesus paid it all, and there is nothing left for me to do.'** *Oh, children, I require you to pick up your cross and to follow Me daily. I require surrender and obedience to My will. My gift of grace is free, but it will cost you all of your sin surrendered and burned up in My Holy Fire. All who have believed the lie that you only need to say a little prayer to be saved will be shocked in this hour as My glory, My presence, and My Fire of Holiness comes with great conviction. Multitudes will finally realize that they have walked the 'broad path' of destruction and will cry out to Me in deep anguish. I am holy—so be ye holy —says your God!"* (See 1 Peter 1:16.)

God's 11th Hour Workers

Hear what King Jesus would say:

"Turnaround, children, turn back to your 'first love.' I am waiting for you...longing for you to come to Me. My arms are open wide, and I will not reject you. Come back; come up and out of the 'pigpen' you have been living in. Come just as you are, and I will wash you, cleanse you with My blood, robe you with fine linen, give to you My 'ring of authority,' and put 'new shoes' on your feet. I will lead and guide you into the fullness that I have for you.

"Everything in your life is going to turn now...a complete turn...a 180-degree turn that will amaze you and even **shock** *you. The change in your life will cause you to weep great tears of joy and of thankfulness. So come, come to the feast I have prepared for you. All of Heaven is rejoicing that you have finally come home to your Father's heart. I've been waiting for you patiently...waiting for you because of My great love for you.*

"You have been longing for Me deep in your heart. I have seen it; I have felt your heart, but you stayed away from Me because of guilt and shame, but now I say: 'Come; I will remove your guilt and the "clothes of shame" that you have worn for so long. Come near to Me, and I will release you from those heavy "chains" that you have been wearing. I will "robe" you with a robe of praise and of thanksgiving. You have cowered before the enemy long enough! It is time to come "home" and to celebrate with Me...with all of Heaven. Enough is enough, child, now move forward into all the glorious things that I have prepared for you!'

"You are My 11th hour worker, and though you have come in late know that you will receive a full reward. I have kept you for this time, for this season, and now you will go forth into the 'harvest field' and 'reap' precious souls for My Kingdom. You wanted this all along, but you didn't know how to reach Me...

how to release the grief and the pain in your heart, and now you will see that with one touch I can lift all of these heavy burdens from your heart.

"Come now; it's turnaround time, a time when everything in your life that has been dark and painful will not only be reversed but burned up in My Holy Fire. Come home to My heart and receive the love and the forgiveness that you have been longing for. Truly, you are My 11th hour worker, and I will send you forth now, and many, many souls will run into My Kingdom because of your glorious testimony and the anointing that is resting upon you—says your God!"

When I was ordained almost 14 years ago, a precious preacher who ministered at my ordination service preached about the 11th hour worker and said that I was one of them. I have ministered at times, but there were never many people that came to these meetings. There was always demonic resistance and a "mountain of difficulty" that would try to prevent me from stepping out in faith. But now I realize that God was in full control all along. Jesus was testing my faith and my trust in Him. He was purifying my heart and my motives and bringing me to the place that it didn't matter if I ministered to one soul or to many. God was strengthening my "inner man" and making me strong, spiritually. I was doing all that Jesus was asking me to do, but I must admit that at times I wondered what I was doing wrong and why I wasn't winning more souls for Jesus, for I loved the Lord deeply and wanted to please Him. I believe that many of God's people have experienced little "fruit" in their lives, but they will now see that God has saved His best for them in these last days.

The Lord has kept me, and many of you, "hidden" for "such a time as this." His desire is to flow through us to bring in this final, end-time harvest. In the "hidden" years God has been purifying our hearts and our motives, filling us with His love, and casting out all fear. He has conformed us more fully into the image of His Son and will soon release us, His 11th hour workers, into the harvest field. God's ways and His timing are always perfect, and He is *never* late.

> You know the saying, "Four months between planting and harvest." But I say, wake up and look around. The fields are already ripe for harvest.
>
> –John 4:35 – NLT

All around us there are hungry and desperate souls who are bound by the evil one and can see no way out of their addictions, perversions, and their deep fears. They feel hopeless and lost and don't know how to reach God. They believe that they have gone too far in their sinful lifestyles and do not realize the deep love that Jesus has for them. In this dark and trying time God is going to "show up" and set multitudes free. He is going to show this world His mercy and grace, but there will be judgment for those who refuse to repent of their rebellion. God will draw souls with strong "cords of love" and will flow through His 11th hour workers in ways that will astound them, the Church, and this world. Now is the time to bring in these precious souls, for the Lord has said: *"The hour is later than we realize!"*

> And about the eleventh hour he went out and found others standing around; and he said to them, "Why have you been standing here idle all day long?" They said to him, "Because no one hired us." He said to them, "You go into the vineyard too." Now when evening came, the owner of the vineyard said to his foreman, "Call the laborers and pay them their wages, starting with the last group to the first." When those hired about the eleventh hour came, each one received a denarius. And so when those hired first came, they thought that they would receive more; but each of them also received a denarius. When they received it, they grumbled at the landowner, saying, "These who were hired last worked only one hour, and you have made them equal to us who have borne the burden of the day's work and the scorching heat." But he answered and said to one of them, "Friend, I am doing you no wrong; did you not agree with me for a denarius? Take what is yours and go; but I want to give to this last

person the same as to you. Is it not lawful for me to do what I want with what is my own? Or is your eye envious because I am generous?" So the last shall be first, and the first, last.
—Matthew 20:6–16 – NASB

I used to think that the workers who were "standing around" were just some "random" people that God will choose in the last days; people who are not yet prepared or seeking the Lord, but now I believe otherwise.

There are many in the Church who believe that their time of usefulness in the Kingdom is over and that they will no longer bear "fruit" for Jesus. They will be surprised and maybe even shocked when Jesus puts His hand on them, "hires" them once again, and sends them forth into the harvest field. These are the ones who don't feel "qualified" or believe that they are too old and too feeble for "active service." They have been "hidden" in the "secret place" with Jesus for years but will now come forth out of "hiding" to complete their calling and their destiny in Christ. They have not been very active in the Church for years, for much of their time has been spent alone with Jesus, praying and just loving on Him.

But now their anointing and calling will be activated powerfully in the Spirit, and they will see that God has prepared their lives for this time and this season in history. A time of refreshing is coming upon those who feel weak and feeble, and many "seniors" will be energized by the Spirit, and they will "mount up with wings as an eagle." God is going to renew their strength, and they will know that God is not "finished" with them but has "recommissioned" them for such a time as this! (See Isaiah 40:31; Esther 4:14.)

I also believe that these 11th hour workers are those who have been or will be radically saved in this season. They feel blessed to be saved but are now standing "idle" because they have not yet heard the call of the Spirit telling them what they are to do and where they are to go. They do not believe that Jesus will "hire" them to bring in this final harvest because of their wicked past, but how wrong they are! They may have been "saved" late, but it is not too late for them to labor in the "field" with Jesus. There will be many 11th hour workers, for God needs all of His faithful ones to work for Him in this final hour, for the harvest will be great. I believe that many of these 11th hour workers, along with His long-time servants, will be martyrs as the end of the age draws near, for they will be willing to give up their very lives for the One they love so passionately!

Jesus is <u>just</u> in **all** of His ways and more generous than we could ever imagine. Everyone who whole-heartedly surrenders to the call of Jesus and who abandons all for Him will receive the same reward, whether they have served Jesus all of their lives or they have come into the Kingdom in a late hour. God's full reward comes to all who are surrendered and are obedient to His will. So, the last will be first, and the first last to show us that we are "equal" in His sight and that God rewards all of His faithful ones who do His will above all. There will be no jealousy or pride in His Kingdom, but we will honor all who have laid down their lives for Jesus. This divine turnaround will actually bring great love and unity into the Body of Christ in this hour.

Jesus recently gave me this powerful *dream* concerning the lateness of the hour. It is time for His 11th hour workers to "punch in" and to release the "greater works" that He wants them to walk in. I know that this dream was not just meant for me but for all of His end-time workers.

In this dream I was at St. Luke's South Shore hospital, where I worked for 25 years, with a friend of mine named "Sandy." After an hour of being trained at the hospital for the new job I was going to do, I was told I could punch in. I wanted to know if they would pay me for the hour of training that I did. Sandy didn't think that we would get paid. I went and stood in line with others by the time clock so that I could "punch in" for work. It was almost time to start my workday, and there was a long line of people ahead of me by the time clock. A lady in front of me was taking quite a long time to punch in, and I was afraid I would be late for work. All of a sudden she stopped what she was doing and held down 2 buttons. Then she told me that I could punch in ahead of her.

In another part of my dream, I saw my "husband," and it looked like he killed a bug that was on a basement wall. I knew that it was the *last* "bug" that needed to be killed. Then, as I thought about my new job, I realized that I did not have time for this hospital job they had trained me for because I was so busy with my other responsibilities at home. I then told my "husband" that I wouldn't be going back to the hospital to work.

Jesus interpreted the dream and told me to look up the meaning of the name "Sandy," and I found out that it means: **Protector of Humanity – Defender of Men.**[xi] Jesus told me that I am called to defend others, to bring the lost and the dying souls around me to Him. In the dream I did not believe that I had the strength to do this because of all my other responsibilities, and I believe that many of God's children feel the same way. Jesus told me that **I** don't have the needed strength in myself but that **He** does. He has all the strength that we need to do what He has called us to do.

This dream was in a hospital setting showing us that there are many "sick" people, both spiritually and physically. God needs His faithful ones to "punch in" and to follow Him into the harvest field. I felt I would punch in late, but I was *right on time.* Some of God's children believe that it is too late for them to follow God's calling, but nothing could be further from the truth. The hour **is** late, but we will "punch in" right on time, and there will be no more delay.

God is bringing me, and you, into a **new place** in Him: into new responsibilities and a place of glorious freedom. We will "punch in," and God will "pay" for all of our "training" and our "wages" as we accomplish His will. We have been *trained* for years, and now our God is calling us to "punch in" and do His works! Now is the time and the season when God will send forth His 11th hour workers into the harvest field. No more will we just "glean" as Ruth did, but we will bring in a great "harvest of souls" and bring them to Jesus. (See Ruth 2:3.) We will no longer gather the "leftovers" but will experience a full and overflowing harvest of souls that will come running into God's Kingdom!

The enemy has taunted and harassed God's people long enough! What has "bugged" us and has weighed us down in this past season will now be lifted from our lives and removed, even as this last "bug" was destroyed in my dream. Jesus, our "Husband," will finish this work quickly inside of us and send us forth in this final hour to complete His work on the earth.

One last thing that I questioned the Lord about was the 2 buttons that this woman held down before I punched in. The Holy Spirit revealed to me the significance of this, and it is most important.

"The number 2 conveys the meaning of a union, division or the verification of facts by witnesses. A man and woman, though two in number, are made one in marriage (Genesis 2:23–24). There is also a union of 2 between Christ and the church (see 1 Corinthians 12)."[xii]

Not only did Jesus show me that those who are in *union* with Him will be His end-time witnesses (see John 17:21–23) but that this union with His true children will *empower* them to do exploits in Him and to set many captives free. We have been prepared and are now being empowered to walk with the Holy Spirit in a way that we have never experienced before. Jesus is placing upon us a fresh anointing and new mantles of power. There are new and greater adventures awaiting us as we step out in faith and onto His "wave of glory!" Now is the time to move forward in the Lord and to ride this "wild wave" with Him! It's time to "PUNCH IN!"

> Therefore, since we are surrounded by such a huge crowd of witnesses to the life of faith, let us strip off every weight that slows us down, especially the sin that so easily trips us up. And let us run with endurance the race God has set before us. We do this by keeping our eyes on Jesus, the Champion who initiates and perfects our faith. Because of the joy awaiting Him, He endured the cross, disregarding its shame. Now He is seated in the place of honor beside God's throne. Think of all the hostility He endured from sinful people; then you won't become weary and give up.
> –Hebrews 12:1–3 – NLT

We are surrounded by a great cloud of witnesses that have gone on home to glory before us, and they are cheering us on and are believing that we are going to "finish our race" victoriously. God is calling His 11th hour workers to shake off every "weight" that is trying to hold us back and to keep us from the fullness of our destiny and calling. God is cutting away the last strongholds and iniquitous "roots" that have "weighed" us down. In the Spirit we will run with endurance and finish our course, and no devil will keep us from the fullness that God has planned for our lives. We are focused and keeping our eyes on Jesus alone. Nothing, no one will distract us from fulfilling our destiny in Jesus. Jesus is our Champion, and He is perfecting our faith so that we can walk in the miraculous! Our heart is set on the joy that is before us, no matter what we have to go through or suffer in this hour! We will never grow weary; we will never give up, for we know that Jesus is our great reward: His love and presence in us throughout eternity!

> Who then can ever keep Christ's love from us? When we have trouble or calamity, when we are hunted down or destroyed, is it because He doesn't love us anymore? And if we are hungry or penniless or in danger or threatened with death, has God deserted us? No, for the Scriptures tell us that for His sake we must be ready to face death at every moment of the day—we are like sheep awaiting slaughter; but despite all this, overwhelming victory is ours through Christ who loved us enough to die for us. For I am convinced that nothing can ever separate us from His love. Death can't, and life can't. The angels won't, and all the powers of hell itself cannot keep God's love away. Our fears for today, our worries about tomorrow, or where we are—high above the sky, or in the deepest ocean—nothing will ever be able to separate us from the love of God demonstrated by our Lord Jesus Christ when He died for us.
> –Romans 8:35–39 – TLB

No matter what we go through, no matter what we suffer in these last days, nothing will weaken our confidence that Jesus is with us and that the Spirit will cover and protect us, even in death. We must be strong warriors in this hour of God's divine turnarounds, for there will be a shaking that none of us have yet seen or experienced on this earth. We will see many painful and heart-wrenching occurrences, but we will stand firm in God's promises just as Mary did and will see the fulfillment of every one of them. Our confidence is strong, and nothing we see, feel, or go through in this late hour will move us. We have grown into strong warriors, and now we know that the powers of hell cannot keep God's love from us! If we are hungry, whether physically or spiritually, God will feed us. In peril or facing imminent death, we will know overwhelming victory in Jesus! No worries or fear will rob us of the love and the joy that we have found in Jesus! What more do we need if the Holy Spirit lives inside of us? We have already entered into eternal life, and no one can take that from us! Nothing will ever separate us from the love of our Savior!

> Therefore do not cast away your confidence, which has great reward. For you have need of endurance, so that after you have done the will of God, you may receive the promise: "For yet a little while, and He who is coming will come and will not tarry. Now the just shall live by faith; but if anyone draws back, My soul has no pleasure in him."
> –Hebrews 10:35–38 – NKJV

We have need of endurance if we are to receive what the Lord has for our lives. In trials and troubles we must stand firm on the promises of God so that we can have *faith for the miraculous*. Without an internal "emptying" of our own will and plans and the sin that so easily entangles us, we cannot, we will not, have the fullness of faith that is required in order to be His 11th hour workers. God will not tarry; He will no longer delay, for this is the time and the season, the decade of the miraculous. God is looking for strong warriors who will not shrink back in fear and unbelief. I want to please Jesus, and I know that you do too, so let's move forward into the fullness that He has for us! Let's receive all of the promises that He has made to us and bring Him the glory that He deserves.

> He made Him who knew no sin to be sin in our behalf, so that we might become the righteousness of God in Him.
> –2 Corinthians 5:21 – NASB

> I have been crucified with Christ; and it is no longer I who live, but Christ lives in me; and the life which I now

live in the flesh I live by faith in the Son of God, who loved me and gave Himself up for me.

–Galatians 2:20

The greatest divine reversal known to man is when Jesus became sin for us, became the ultimate sacrifice, so that we could be freed from sin and iniquity, be conformed into the image of Christ, and be filled with His righteousness. Jesus ratified the blood covenant through His death on the cross so that our sin could be washed away. (See Matthew 26:28.) In order for this to be "worked out" in our lives, there must be a binding agreement, a sacrifice of our lives to Jesus so that we can come into the *full* blessings of His covenant. Being crucified with Christ must be more than just *head* knowledge; it must be something that we *experience* through the power of the Spirit. As we yield to the Holy Spirit and allow Him to cut away all that is unholy, we will then know the power of the covenant in our lives. Many believe that this will happen only when we die, but the *transforming process* begins as soon as we come to Jesus and surrender all to Him. What could be more glorious than this?

We are in covenant with Christ. But covenants are no longer a widespread practice, and many Christians do not realize what exactly it entails. According to Jewish Jewels a covenant "is a solemn, binding agreement entered into by two parties. The Hebrew word for covenant is b'rit (b'reet) which literally means 'cutting,' and implies making an incision until blood flows. A covenant is the most sacred of all binding contracts."[xiii]

God is calling His end-time workers to embrace the cross of Christ daily and to follow Jesus wherever He would lead us. As God's 11th hour workers, when we truly realize that we have been crucified with Christ, we will no longer live for ourselves, in our own will and desires. The New Covenant is a "better" covenant in that now God is the One who works in us "both to will and to do for His good pleasure." (See Hebrews 8:6; Philippians 2:13.) It is no longer God's people trying to earn His favor by doing good works and cleaning up their lives in their own strength. We now live by faith in the Son of God as a "living sacrifice" for Him. Christ has become our righteousness, for we have "cut a covenant" with Him and have surrendered *all* to His Lordship. All that we *have* and all that we *are* in this covenant relationship belongs to Jesus, and all that He *has* and all that He *is* belongs to us in glorious exchange. What a glorious divine reversal! I can now be released from my sin and my shame and be filled with Jesus' life and righteousness!

A beautiful example of a covenantal relationship is the friendship that David and Johnathan had as found in 1 Samuel 18:1, 3–4 (ESV): *"As soon as he had finished speaking to Saul, the soul of Jonathan was knit to the soul of David, and Jonathan loved him as his own soul...Then Jonathan made a covenant with David, because he loved him as his own soul. And Jonathan stripped himself of the robe that was on him and gave it to David, and his armor, and even his sword and his bow and his belt."*

Here we see that their hearts became one with each other, and this is what happens when we "cut a covenant" with our Beloved Savior. We will not withhold one thing from Jesus, no matter what He asks of us. We love Him more than we love our own lives. Johnathan gave David his coat, battle clothes, sword, bow, and belt; in the same way we give Jesus *all* that we have, everything that we are holding onto in this world, in order to show Him that we trust Him implicitly. We trust that Jesus will defend us and keep us safe in all the battles we encounter in this life even as Jonathan was trusting David with his future, knowing that David would become king and would always defend him. Jesus has now become our All-in-All, and nothing will separate us from His love.

As I was writing about the covenant, God reminded me of what Simeon spoke to Mary concerning the "sword" that would enter her heart. Mary's heart bled as she was "cut" deeply throughout her life in her covenantal relationship with her God, but she also experienced the fullness of the Lord's blessings in her life. In the same way as we follow Jesus all the way, we, too, will experience "cuttings" as sin and the shame of our past is cut away from our hearts and our lives. Our hearts will bleed, but they will be healed in His love. In this glorious relationship with our covenant-keeping God, nothing will be withheld from us, and we will come into a deep love relationship with our Creator God! When we "cut a covenant" with our God, it is then that our hearts become one with Him, and we will *experience,* because of what our Savior accomplished for us on the cross and through the glorious power of His resurrection, the fullness of His blessing.

Before I close this chapter, I want to share another dream concerning God's 11th hour "harvesters" and how it is time for a great turnaround in our lives. Again, I do not believe that this dream was only for me but for all who are "called" in this final hour.

In this dream I was behind the wheel in my car, and it was dark. I mentioned to my husband that I couldn't see well at night. When I started to drive I crashed into a blue "International Harvester" classic car. When I looked at the vehicle I hit, I saw that the driver's side was smashed in. Then I noticed that the blue paint on the car looked old and that it was peeling off. I looked and saw a man, the "owner" of the car, and he was just standing there smiling. He looked so calm. I started looking for my "American Family" insurance card, but I couldn't find it. I thought to myself in the dream that the "man" was happy because he thought that my insurance would pay for a whole new paint job for His "Harvester."

I remember feeling very depressed in this dream, and I no longer cared about anything in my life. I had completely given up on ever seeing my dreams come to pass. The blows had been many in my life, and I no longer wanted to go on living. To say that I was discouraged is an understatement, for when my husband started to tell me about the insurance covering the vehicle, I didn't even want to hear about it.

God showed me that many of His children are in the dark concerning their calling and destiny and that He is the "owner" of the car, which represents our ministry and our destiny in Christ; Jesus is the great "International Harvester." Many of His children are depressed because of the long delay. (See Proverbs 13:12.) They are in a "dark" place and cannot see where the Spirit is leading them. They have been driving in the dark and have "crashed," and they feel that they may never see the fulfillment of the promises that God has made for them. Many 11th hour workers feel this way and have grown deeply discouraged. They are standing "idle" and do not believe that they will be "hired" by the Lord. Even as the blue paint on the "harvester," blue standing for a *heavenly* ministry,[xiv] was peeling off so they believe that their destiny is now "fading away." They believe their "destiny vehicle" is an "antique," old and worn and will never be "restored." Nothing could be further from the truth! Remember: You are one of a kind, a "classic" in God's sight!

The driver's side had taken a "hit," showing that the enemy has come against God's children, trying to not only delay their calling but to destroy the ministry that God has "birthed" in them. The "owner" was calm and smiling; Jesus is in full control of what has happened and is happening in our lives, and He is our "American Insurance."

The meaning of *insurance* in the English Dictionary is: "*a practice or arrangement by which a company or government agency provides a guarantee of compensation for specified loss, damage, illness, or death in return for payment of a premium.*"[xv] Jesus is our "insurance agent," and He has already paid **all** of our premiums through the blood of His cross. Jesus will "restore" and refresh His people who have "crashed," for truly, even now, He is making "all things new" in our lives. I also believe that **America** has been called to bring in a "harvest of souls" in this hour—multiplied millions who are lost in this generation. Satan has tried to destroy our nation, but God's plan and destiny for our nation will come to pass. Our forefathers made powerful covenants with God, and He has not forgotten them. There are many in this hour who are in covenant with Jesus and have surrendered all to Him. Jesus has a faithful remnant in this nation that will fulfill His will on the earth.

My husband has a 1948 classic car, an International Harvester. When my husband bought this vehicle, God spoke to me and told me that I would go to the nations and reap a harvest of souls. My name, Theresa, means: **To reap, to gather in, harvester.**[xvi] I've always loved the meaning of my name. I have waited long for the fulfillment of God's promises to come to pass just as, I believe, some of you have. But know this: There is a fresh anointing being released on God's 11th hour workers in this hour, a stronger and more powerful anointing that will break the enemy's "yoke of bondage" off of the souls and lives of millions who are walking in darkness.

In this dream I had finally let go of trying to "fix" things in my own strength and wisdom. I had let go of everything, even my very life, and Jesus told me that this is right where He wants me in this hour. All of the trials, all of the suffering that His 11th hour workers have gone through has accomplished what God has been after all along: **a total letting go of our lives and a full trust in what He alone can accomplish in our lives.** I believe that many of God's children are in this place and will find out that in all of their "dying" the life of Jesus is now coming forth in and through them in abundance. They will see that nothing that they've gone through has been in vain.

Sometimes what we have held onto, our deepest dreams and desires, must be sacrificed back to the Lord even as Abraham laid his son Isaac, the promised child, on the altar and gave him back to God. (See Genesis 22:1–18.) Our God is a "jealous" God, and Jesus must be our "first love," for He will never take 2nd place in our lives. (See Exodus 34:14.) The Lord is after our hearts, and He will not allow any other "loves" before Him, not even our ministry, our destiny child in Him. Our God passionately loves us, and He will make sure that our love relationship with Him is the most important thing in our lives. When Jesus is "enough" for us and we know that nothing else in this world can or will satisfy us, He will then release the fullness of His "promises" to us, for only then can we be trusted to walk in His power and not succumb to pride and fall into the "traps" of the enemy. As we surrender ALL no money and no pleasures on this earth will be able to draw us away from Jesus.

Like Joseph of old sometimes our dreams have to "die" before they are resurrected. God gave Joseph some powerful promises through his dreams, but little did he realize how long it would take to bring them to fruition. He did not see the painful years ahead: his brother's betrayal, being thrown into a "pit," being sold into slavery, being falsely accused by Potiphar's wife, and then being thrown into prison for years. (Genesis 37:23–28; 39:11–13.)

Joseph didn't realize that he was being "groomed" through much suffering to become 2nd to Pharoah, and because of the gift God had given him in being able to interpret dreams, his "suddenly" finally arrived. (See Genesis 41:1–43.) Do you think that Joseph didn't struggle through these years of *seeming* denial…when it looked like the promises that God made to him had fallen to the ground? There had to be times when he thought that the dreams the Lord gave him would never come to pass, but still, he held onto them. I believe that Joseph grew mightily in faith through all of his pain and his struggles and that nothing he went through was wasted.

Joseph went from the "pit" to the "palace" because he kept his focus on God and not on his circumstances. He didn't know when or how God would accomplish these promises in his life, but he knew that his God was faithful; he knew that the Lord would come through for him. In the same way the Lord's faithful warriors who would not let go of His promises will now experience God's divine turnaround. Their "suddenly" has arrived, and they will stand in awe as the Lord moves mightily on their behalf.

In another part of the dream, I had "bedding" that I wanted to wash, but the washer and dryer were being used. When I came back later I saw that the woman who was using them had completed her "wash." I watched her as she took out of the washer a wooden frame with "antique" pictures in it. She was so happy that she was able to "clean" these pictures.

Jesus is working diligently to cleanse our *bloodline* and to prepare us, His 11th hour workers, to bring in a glorious harvest of souls in this hour. The "antique" pictures represented our past: all of the sins and the iniquities in our bloodline and the ancestral "curses" that have kept us from the *fullness* that God has for us. All of this is being removed in the power of His blood. We will experience *full* freedom in the Spirit, the "abundant life" that Jesus promised us in His Word. (See John 10:10.)

Your ministry in Jesus may have taken a hard "hit" from the enemy, but you must **believe** and **know** without a doubt that God will restore it back to you 100-fold. You may be in a "dark" place right now and can't see what the Lord is doing, but you must **believe** that Jesus is in full control of your life and that He will bring you through into His glorious Light! Not only will you and your ministry in Jesus be "resurrected" but God will restore your family (American Family) and give you "joy unspeakable and full of glory!" You are God's "harvester," God's 11th hour worker, and you *will* finish your race, and many will say to you: *"Blessed is she who believed that He would fulfill His promises to her!"*

Hear what the Spirit is saying:

> *"Your nation will turn back to Me, and I say: 'Many are already "turning" because of the exposure of evil that millions are seeing. Not only are their eyes opening but their hearts are opening to Truth, and this is the first step in coming home to My heart. I am after souls in this hour, and in this great reversal and turnaround, multitudes will run into My Kingdom.'*

"There is a 'Mighty Force' working in this hour, and it is the power of My Holy Spirit moving across the nations of this earth. This is not an isolated movement but a movement that will release not only multitudes of souls but even the very governments of the earth. My people are rising up now in great strength and power, and nothing, no one, will stop this glorious movement.

"My people have seen enough, felt enough pain and grief in this hour, and they are now rising up and taking the 'Land.' No one will stop this movement of My people in the power of the Holy Spirit until all lines up with My sovereign will.

"This turnaround and divine reversal are coming forth quickly, and it has begun. Now you will see it come forth in fullness and in power, and My people will take the 'Land'; they will bring souls into My Kingdom and even turn the governments around and back to righteousness and My divine order in this very hour.

"This is the time and the season you have waited for, some of you for a long, long time, and now I say: 'My hidden ones come forth, for I have saved you for this time and season. You have been hidden in a dark place, in a "cave" of isolation and pain, but I am now calling you to come forth. You have been like Lazarus in a "tomb of darkness," pain, fear, and unbelief, but I am now calling you forth into My Light and Glory, and you will be My end-time witness.'

"So come; come children, out of your graves of loss, dryness, and even spiritual 'deadness.' I will now resurrect you and bring you into the very fullness that I have for you. You are My 'Lazarus Company' that I will send forth to turn this world right-side up. The dark will become light and the grief and pain that you have been carrying will turn into rejoicing as you come out of your 'graves of death' and into My glorious light and resurrection power.

"Now is the time when you will walk in the miraculous. You will have faith because of what you have suffered to believe for the miraculous...for impossible situations, even the raising of the *dead! Because of what you have been through, because you have held onto the 'rope of faith' in your 'seeming' impossible situations, now I will flow through you to save millions, and even cities, states, and nations across the face of this earth will have a glorious turnaround and come back to the path of righteousness in this hour. Cities will be 'lit' with the Light and Glory of My presence, and untold millions of souls will run to My 'throne of grace.'*

"Trust Me now and walk with Me, for I will anoint you to 'break the yoke' off of those who are bound, and you will never be the same, but will walk as that 'new man' in Me, created in Me for good works—says your God!" (See Ephesians 2:10.)

Chapter 4
The Upper Room of Power

A New Anointing — A New Day!

A new anointing for a new day
Oh Lord let it pour
A new anointing for a new day
To carry the glory of the Lord
To carry the glory of the Lord

The oil from yesterday has gone stale
And the strength that I once trusted in has failed
But Your fresh Word has been spoken
And my proud heart has been broken
So once again I come behind the veil
(asking for)

A new anointing for a new day

Oh Holy Fragrance Sweet Perfume
All Consuming Fire fill this room
No more living in yesterday's grace
Oh Lord pour Your Power
And your Passion for
Your Purposes today
(We receive)

A new anointing for a new day[xvii]

There is a powerful new anointing coming upon God's people, a fresh anointing that will awaken God's people to the fullness that He has prepared for their lives. It is not that God's true children aren't anointed, but there is a stronger, more powerful anointing that is coming so that His people can stand strong in the days ahead. This anointing is going to break the hearts of God's wayward children and bring a fire of repentance that will unify His children, one to another, and fill them with His fiery love. Proud hearts will be broken and will be filled with the life and the humility of Jesus. A spirit of unity is coming to the Body of Christ along with the Spirit's "Holy Fire" that will release God's healing power and deliverance to this generation.

Those who have felt their weakness and have realized that the anointing they once enjoyed has grown "stale" will now be revitalized in this glorious new anointing from on High. They have stood on His promises for so long that many of God's children have grown weary and need the *refreshing waters* of the Spirit to once again fill them.

We are called to be "carriers of His glory," and this stronger and more glorious anointing will fill us with the very fullness of the "Living Christ." Jesus will live His Life through His surrendered ones, and all will know that He is alive and well and on the move in this very hour. No longer will God's children live a selfish and self-centered life, just barely holding on until Jesus comes. This anointing will free God's people *first,* and then the multitudes will run to Jesus in this last great outpouring of God's glory.

Fresh prophetic words have been released from Heaven, and many are now lifting their faces to Jesus and receiving the fullness of His Life that they have so longed for. They have picked up their cross and are following their Savior daily, and because of their obedience they are now entering into a place of deepest intimacy with their Savior, moving "behind the veil," and gazing upon the face of their Beloved Jesus. They have smelled the fragrance of His sweet perfume, His very presence, and have known Him as a "consuming fire," burning up all of their sin and their iniquity. Jesus is now their "All in All."

They no longer live in yesterday's grace, for in this dark hour they needed a greater portion of His love and mercy. They have found it in this new anointing, this greater release of His Spirit in and through them. Now they walk in the full Life of Jesus and in that High and Holy Place with Him. They have only **one** desire, **one** passion, and that is to do the Father's will and to accomplish His purposes on this earth! Thank you, Jesus, for this new day; this glorious "Great Awakening" that is now being poured forth into the earth!

> He has made everything beautiful and appropriate in its time.
> –Ecclesiastes 3:11a (AMP)

Jesus is the One who makes everything beautiful in *His* perfect timing, *not ours*. I believe that this is where many of God's children have failed to trust Him completely, for when Jesus doesn't come through for them in their *timing* and their *way*, they get offended. God has an *order*, and He also has a *process* that He must take His people through in order to get their hearts right with Him so that they can receive from Him with an *open* heart. At times God's people will experience an "instant" miracle of healing or deliverance, but this is not the norm. Many in the Church compare themselves with other saints of God, how the Lord is working in *their* lives and blessing them, and they expect the same "treatment."

We are unique individuals, and God does not work the same way in any two of His children. Our backgrounds, upbringing, experiences, generational bondages and propensities, all of these and more are factors in how the Lord will deal with us as individuals. You and I should never compare ourselves with anyone else, and it is wrong to do so. As I was growing spiritually I compared myself to others many times, and it stirred up deep anger in my heart and deepest jealousy. When I saw others being blessed when all I felt was pain, it angered me. I was angry with God, others, and especially with myself. We must keep our eyes on Jesus and our hearts set on Him alone so that we can be transformed spiritually and can find out what He has for our lives *personally*.

Strengthen the exhausted, and make the feeble strong. Say to those with anxious heart, "Take courage, fear not. Behold, your God will come with vengeance; the retribution of God will come, but He will save you." Then the eyes of those who are blind will be opened, and the ears of those who are deaf will be unstopped. Then those who limp will leap like a deer, and the tongue of those who cannot speak will shout for joy. For waters will burst forth in the wilderness, and streams in the desert.

–Isaiah 35:3–6 – NASB

Thousands, if not millions, of God's children have grown weary these past years because of continual warfare and the fiery trials that they have gone through, but this new and greater anointing that is now being released from the Spirit of God will refresh and will renew them inwardly. Even their bodies will experience new strength and vitality. These are "times of refreshing," and all who have experienced weariness and pain can now come to these refreshing "waters" and receive an anointing from on High that will break every yoke and every bondage off of their lives.

This is NOT the time to give up, but a time to know that your suffering has not been in vain. I say to you: *"Take courage and fear not, for your God is coming with a vengeance, and He will save not only you from the deep waters you have walked in but also your loved ones who have known demonic attack and have grown weary in their battles."* Jesus is going to restore families in this hour in miraculous ways that will astound us!

It's a new day! And in this day both the spiritual and physical senses will be healed: blinded eyes will now be opened; deafened ears will be unstopped; those that "limp" will now leap for joy, and the "dumb" will shout the praises of God! All that has been barren and dry, spiritually, will now be flooded with the glory of the Lord! It's time to rejoice saints of God, for this new day has already begun!

It shall come to pass in that day that his burden will be taken away from your shoulder, and his yoke from your neck, and the yoke will be destroyed because of the anointing oil.

–Isaiah 10:27 – NKJV

God is lifting and breaking off the heavy burdens that His people have carried for so long. This greater anointing in this new day will crush and will demolish their *afflictions* in the power of the Holy Spirit. Because God's faithful ones have been carrying their "cross" and following the Lord daily, resurrection power will now be released in its fullness in and through their lives. They will know that their NEW DAY has arrived. They will walk in greater power and authority, and no devil in hell will ever cause them to fear again, for the love of the Father will fill them to overflowing and cast out all fear!

> Do not remember the former things, or ponder the things of the past. Listen carefully, I am about to do a new thing, now it will spring forth; will you not be aware of it? I will even put a road in the wilderness, rivers in the desert.
>
> –Isaiah 43:18–19 – AMP

This is the day and the hour when deep rooted iniquities will be pulled up and out of the hearts of millions. The "former things" that have troubled our hearts will now be released from our lives, never to trouble us again. Jesus is doing a *new thing* in this generation, in this season of glory, and what has looked impossible to change in our lives, our families, the Church, and this world will now be changed in His glory forever.

Will we be aware of it? Or will we turn, harden our hearts, and believe that God will not change our lives and this world according to His will and His plan? I believe it will be so powerful that no one will be able to deny what God is doing unless they deliberately turn their backs on Him and refuse to believe that these changes are coming from His Mighty Hand. God is looking for open hearts so that He can pour His glory in and through His people in ways that will astound this world, but we must be willing to embrace these new things and the drastic changes that may be required in order to receive this fullness.

> He put a new song in my mouth, a song of praise to our God; many will see and fear [with great reverence] and will trust confidently in the Lord.
>
> –Psalm 40:3

> O sing to the Lord a new song, for He has done marvelous and wonderful things; His right hand and His holy arm have gained the victory for Him.
>
> –Psalm 98:1

This world will stand in awe and wonder as they see what is taking place on this earth. Many will "see and fear" as they watch this end-time drama unfold and witness signs and wonders that will take their breath away! Not only is there a new anointing for a new day but there will come forth from God's people a *new song*...a song of praise so loud and so powerful that all will hear of what our Mighty King is accomplishing for His people. All will see that God's children are blessed in the midst of great chaos and the judgments of God. They will see the Lord's children filled with overflowing joy even in the midst of overwhelming darkness, and they will wonder at the magnitude of what God is doing in their midst.

> The people who walk in darkness shall see a great Light—a Light that will shine on all those who live in the land of the shadow of death. For Israel will again be great, filled with joy like that of reapers when the harvesttime has come, and like that of men dividing up the plunder they have won. For God will break the chains that bind His people and the whip that scourges them, just as He did when He destroyed the vast host of the Midianites by Gideon's little band.
>
> –Isaiah 9:2–4 – TLB

So many are living in the "valley of the shadow of death" spiritually, but now they will see the brightness of the glory of God shining in and through His true children in this very hour. His people will be filled with heavenly joy, a lasting joy that this earth can never produce. So many of God's people have been saddened and depressed because of all that has taken place in these past years, but that is all changing as we see our God move in astounding ways…ways that our hearts could never fully fathom. Now the "harvest" is coming in, and God's children will see that what they have gone through has prepared them to be Jesus' "nets" to draw in the lost and the dying. Now we are taking back **all** that the enemy has stolen from us!

God used Gideon and a small band of 300 warriors in order to release His judgment against the Midianites. (See Judges 7:1–25.) This represents God's end-time remnant that have been tested and prepared for this very season. These are the Lord's "trumpets" and "broken pitchers" who have *faith for the miraculous*. The Midianites turned on each other and slaughtered themselves, and I believe that we will see something similar as God's hand moves against those who are coming against His people and His plans in this hour.

> Jabez cried out to the God of Israel, saying, "Oh that You would indeed bless me and enlarge my border [property], and that Your hand would be with me, and You would keep me from evil so that it does not hurt me!" And God granted his request.
> –1 Chronicles 4:10 – AMP

> Enlarge the place of your tent, and let them stretch out the curtains of your dwellings; do not spare; lengthen your cords, and strengthen your stakes.
> –Isaiah 54:2 – NKJV

God is enlarging our *influence* in this hour and is opening many doors before us. The Spirit recently spoke to our prayer and Bible study group and said: *"You will not have to 'kick' open doors of opportunity in this season, for I will open them up before you!"* We have been passionate to have more opportunities to reach the lost and the dying, and as the Lord has been "stretching" our hearts so now are we prepared to bring in this final harvest. In every fulfilled promise that Jesus has made to us, we will see an enlarging of our "border," our inheritance in Him. Jesus is enlarging us in *every* area of our lives: in healing, in power, monetarily, spiritually, and in freedom and liberty, bringing us into the abundant life that He has promised us. Not one area of our lives will be left untouched. Jesus is our Rock and our Refuge, and in the midst of great troubles He will be our "Hiding Place." (See Psalm 91:1–16.)

> But my horn [my emblem of strength and power] You have exalted like that of a wild ox; I am anointed with fresh oil [for Your service].
> –Psalm 92:10 – AMP

This new anointing, this greater anointing will be an emblem of the Spirit's strength in His overcomers, His warriors, in this *decade of power*. God has given His people an inward strength to overcome every obstacle that the enemy has placed before them. They will be seen as a "force" that no devil and no man will be able to stop. This double portion anointing that is now being released will be known for its strength and its power to walk in the miraculous and to see impossible situations overturned for our good and for the glory of God! Miracles, signs, and wonders will now be commonplace as our King moves in unprecedented ways! A new, fresh anointing for a new day; it has arrived!

Jesus our King says:

> *"There is a new, fresh, more powerful anointing coming upon, in, and through My 'chosen ones' in this hour. This anointing will break the 'yoke' off of many, many souls as My Spirit moves in power in this very hour of darkness.*
>
> *"I have prepared you, children, for this very time and season to move with Me in new and even* **unusual** *ways, for what is coming to your nation and this world will require a greater power to rest in and upon you in order to overcome the 'hordes of hell' that are being released.*

"I have set you free, and I have set you in a High Place in Me, and you will not be moved neither will you be frightened by the things that you see happening all around you. You will remember Psalm 91, and you will speak it daily over your life, your family, your loved ones, and the nations of this world.

"My precious children, you are the ones I have called to move with Me in this final hour. Like Peter you have come out of your 'boat of comfort' and are walking on 'water' with Me. But I say: 'You will not take your eyes off of Me and look at the "waves" around you neither will you allow the "winds of destruction" to move you. You will not "sink" in these "troubled waters," I promise you. We will walk together hand in hand, and My Spirit will support you on every side. You will know that you are not alone, and you will joy in the God of your salvation. Come close, and you will hear Me whispering to you. You will feel My deep, intimate touch, and you will know that you will never fear again, come hell or high water.'

"The 'rescue mission' has begun, and you are an integral part of what I am doing in this world in this very hour. You have a place and a position in Me that no other can have...a place of power and of authority in Me that will now be released in and through your life. This new and fresh anointing will change you **internally** and set many captives free. What you have experienced in Me in the past is 'stale.' You have stepped into a new day...a glorious day of freedom and of liberty in My Spirit. There is now coming upon you an anointing from on High that will release inside of you a boldness and a power that you have never known, and you will wonder in awe because of the inner strength you will now feel and the boldness and the power that will be released through you to the nations.

"You are strong, My chosen ones, and for this very season I have prepared and have conditioned you to be My end-time witnesses, and you will never be moved again!"

The Release of the Holy Spirit's Power

This generation of *true* Believer's are being anointed with a double portion of the Holy Spirit's power, for it is needed in order to walk as an overcomer in this dark hour. The spiritual warfare is intense, but God has a "prepared people" who have learned to walk in the High Place of power with Him. They have learned, through many fiery trials, how to use their "weapons of war" and to overcome the darkness that has come against them. (See 2 Corinthians 10:3–6.) They are anointed with the Holy Spirit's power and presence and are able to complete the mission that God has ordained them to walk in. In this season we will see and will experience a greater release of the Holy Spirit's power!

> For God has not given us a spirit of fear, but of power and of love and of a sound mind.
> –2 Timothy 1:7 – NKJV

No more will God's children walk in fear and in timidity, for those days are forever gone! There are explosions of power being released on the inside of God's anointed ones, and they will walk in the love and the passion of their Savior, and multitudes will be released from their "yokes of bondage." These impassioned ones have spent years walking with their Savior and have disciplined their lives to obey the Lord fully. Their minds have been renewed in God's Word, and they have been freed from the "traps" of the enemy. They hear the voice of the Spirit clearly and have learned to take the lies and the thoughts of the enemy into "captivity." (See 2 Corinthians 10:5.)

> THE SPIRIT OF THE LORD IS UPON ME (the Messiah), BECAUSE HE HAS ANOINTED ME TO PREACH THE GOOD NEWS TO THE POOR. HE HAS SENT ME TO ANNOUNCE RELEASE (pardon, forgiveness) TO THE CAPTIVES, AND RECOVERY OF SIGHT TO THE BLIND, TO SET FREE THOSE WHO ARE OPPRESSED (downtrodden, bruised, crushed by tragedy).
> –Luke 4:18 – AMP

The Spirit has anointed His end-time warriors in order for them to have the strength and the power to preach the Good News to all who are desperately searching for Truth. These bold ones will release God's pardon and forgiveness to those who feel hopeless and who believe that they can never be released from their "prison of sin." Millions need to be set free from addictions and from perversions so strong that only the power of the Spirit can free them, and this is why we need a greater and a stronger anointing from on High. So many are spiritually blind; so many are oppressed, crushed, and bruised by the evil one, but this greater anointing will free these captives, these "slaves" of satan. The enemy has tried to stop this next glorious awakening and outpouring of the Spirit, but he will not prevail in doing so. Our God is on the move, and nothing, no one will stop our King Jesus!

> For His divine power has granted to us everything pertaining to life and godliness, through the true knowledge of Him who called us by His own glory and excellence. Through these He has granted to us His precious and magnificent promises, so that by them you may become partakers of the divine nature, having escaped the corruption that is in the world on account of lust.
> –2 Peter 1:3–4 – NASB

We have everything that we need to overcome the powers of darkness in this present age. In the Spirit of Truth and the power of the Holy Spirit, we have received a greater anointing and a revelation of who we truly are in Christ. Now we know that we have the power and the authority in Jesus to decree and to release His will and His desires into the earth. We have become partakers of His divine nature, and nothing will be withheld from us, for all things belong to us in Jesus. We are walking in openness and in obedience with our King, and His will is our will; all that we ask of Him will be given to us.

Now we have a *true* knowledge of who Jesus is: not just a meek and mild Savior but the glorious King of the Universe, the Lion of Judah who has established His throne in the heavens and whose Kingdom rules over all! (See Psalm 103:19.) God has granted to us His magnificent promises, but we must *stand on them* and *receive them* no matter what warfare and lies from the enemy come against us. We must never let go of these promises, for as we receive them the nature of Jesus fills us to overflowing, and we will walk in this greater anointing.

> And I will ask the Father, and He will give you another Helper (Comforter, Advocate, Intercessor—Counselor, Strengthener, Standby), to be with you forever—the Spirit of Truth, whom the world cannot receive [and take to its heart] because it does not see Him or know Him, but you know Him because He (the Holy Spirit) remains with you continually and will be in you...But the Helper (Comforter, Advocate, Intercessor—Counselor, Strengthener, Standby), the Holy Spirit, whom the Father will send in My name [in My place, to represent Me and act on My behalf], He will teach you all things. And He will help you remember everything that I have told you.
> –John 14:16–17, 26 – AMP

The Holy Spirit was sent to this earth over 2,000 years ago on the Day of Pentecost, and He will not leave this earth until He fulfills His *full* will in and through our lives. He is our Comforter, Advocate, Strengthener, and Intercessor, and He represents Jesus and acts on His behalf and teaches us *all* things. The Spirit is the One who brings back to our remembrance every word, every promise that Jesus has ever spoken to us. The Holy Spirit is the "Spirit of Truth" and will never lead us astray. We are sanctified, made holy through God's "baptism of fire," the fire of the "Living Christ" and the Truth of God's Word.

We see and know Jesus because of the abiding presence of His Spirit in us. God's Spirit is the One who anoints us with Holy Fire; He leads us and guides us into all that Jesus and the Father have planned for our lives. Without the power of the Holy Spirit's anointing, we would never be able to walk in the fullness of our calling and our destiny. Thank You, Holy Spirit, for your glorious presence in our lives!

> In the last day, that great day of the feast, Jesus stood and cried out, saying, If any man thirsts, let him come unto Me and drink. He that believes in Me, as the Scripture has said, out of his belly shall flow rivers of living water.
> –John 7:37–38 – Jubilee Bible 2000

Jesus is calling out to those who are "thirsty" for His presence in this generation. He is crying out to the downcast and the downtrodden ones who feel hopeless and alone. It is a cry from His heart of compassion, and if you could feel His broken heart, you would weep with Him. It is a cry from deep within His heart as He looks at those who are bound with the tormenting thoughts of the evil one and the "strongholds" that only Jesus can free them from.

Jesus longs to fill His people with the power of the Holy Spirit so that these "Rivers" can flow through them to those who are dying of spiritual thirst. Without these refreshing waters from the Spirit of God, we will remain powerless and ineffective in this generation. Without the infilling of the Spirit, we will never experience the transforming power of our God and will never make a difference in our generation. We need to cry out to our God to empower us with this greater and more powerful anointing so that millions can be set free from their besetting sins and iniquities. This can only be accomplished as we surrender *all* to Jesus and allow the Spirit to have His way in our lives.

> But when the Holy Spirit has come upon you, you will receive power to testify about Me with great effect, to the people in Jerusalem, throughout Judea, in Samaria, and to the ends of the earth, about My death and resurrection.
> –Acts 1:8 – TLB

> Then he said, "This is God's message to Zerubbabel: 'Not by might, nor by power, but by My Spirit, says the Lord Almighty—you will succeed because of My Spirit, though you are few and weak.'"
> –Zechariah 4:6

God has a word that He would speak to His remnant in this hour: *"Though you are weak and few in number, know that your God will come through for you. He will lift you up to a High Place of glory and remove every 'restriction' that the enemy has placed upon your life. Though you are few in number, you will now do exploits in My name. You will succeed; you will not fail to complete the mission that I have called you to complete in Me. Do not look at your weakness or your own ability, but know that you have been empowered by My Spirit to move with Me and to take new territories in My name. You have found that in your weakness, I have been your strength. I have anointed you with a new anointing for a new day of glory and of power, and now you will walk on the 'High Road of Holiness' with the Lord your God."*

Without the power of the Holy Spirit in our lives, we will accomplish very little in this hour. A dream that the Lord gave me while writing this section shows us how desperately we need the Holy Spirit's power and "refining fire" in our lives if we are to enter into the fullness of His anointing and the promises that He has given to us.

In this dream I was on the "outskirts" of Israel, the *Promised Land*, with a few other people. A "man" told us to come to his house when we arrived, but when we called him after our arrival, he wasn't home. When we finally got ahold of him, he told us that his "wife" would be home and that she would "feed" us. We were driving in a car, and as I looked back I saw a couple of people that left their car and decided to pedal on a tandem bicycle. When I looked at them, they were far behind us, and I wondered if they would ever catch up to us.

In another part of my dream, I saw myself and others at a banquet in a large building, and I had some "fried" food on my plate. I then saw a delicious looking *piece of cake,* and I was so happy to get the *last* piece. A young man came over and saw that there was no more cake, and he was upset.

I then saw a long line of people that had to go through a *security check line* (like an airport security checkpoint) to be "cleared" in order to proceed into the "Promised Land." The people I traveled with had to show the security guards some kind of "receipt." We went back to another building to look for their *receipts* so they could get the clearance needed to get through *security*. We looked all over for these *passes*, but because it was dark in the area where we were looking, we could not find them. We pulled up a shade, but it was still dark. They continued to look for these *receipts,* but they could not find them.

I knew that I had what I needed, my *receipt,* but then I wondered if maybe I had put *their* receipts in *my* purse. I thought about my purse and started to look for it. I couldn't remember where I placed it, and I asked a young man if he knew where it was. He told me where my purse was, and I saw that it was next to another purse. I grabbed it and thought to myself that I had better hold onto it tightly and not let it out of my sight.

Jesus told me that this dream represents the "promises" that He has given *me* and given *you* in this hour. The "cake" represented that a special time of celebration is coming to those who have been through the "fire" of the Holy Spirit (the fried food). Jesus also revealed to me that this has been a *time of testing* for His Church. The "man" that was not "home" represented Jesus, and He has *tested* His people to see if they would *continue* to believe and to stand on His promises in the midst of *adverse circumstances,* much like the Gideon army was tested and narrowed down to 300 warriors.

Those who were with me wanted to "sup" with this "man," but he told us that his "wife" would feed us. The *wife* in my dream represented the *bride of Christ,* and Jesus has been speaking through her, His prophets, in this hour, but few have eaten the "food" that she has been giving to them. This has been a *great test* for the Body of Christ, and many have failed to listen to what God is speaking through His true prophets concerning what is happening in this nation and on the earth. There is a company of true prophets and teachers speaking and teaching Truth in this hour, but many have maligned and mocked them, and Jesus is not pleased with this.

Those who were riding the tandem *bicycle* are those who are working in their *own strength and power.* They are trying to accomplish God's will in their own way and in their own understanding. These are the ones who are trying to receive the promises of God through the "works of the law," by their own good works and efforts. They do not have the Holy Spirit's power that is needed to get into the "Promised Land" and to receive the promises of God. I also remember saying that we needed a *guide* to lead us *through* the Promised Land and that "Guide" is the Holy Spirit, for we can do nothing apart from Him.

A **security check**, according to Collins Dictionary, is *"1. The process of checking that a person is not armed, or carrying something dangerous. 2. A verification of somebody's identity and trustworthiness."*[xviii]

Jesus told me that those who are going forth in ministry in their own strength will never get through the "security check," for they have not submitted their lives to the Holy Spirit's "refining fire" in this hour. In this "security check" the Holy Spirit will look deep inside our hearts to see if there is any "hidden" sin or anything idolatrous or dark. This is the season when the Holy Spirit is shining His Light deep into our hearts and removing what is not of Him. My "purse" represented my *identity in Christ,* and we must cling to who we are in Jesus so that no devil will rob us of our true identity. The lies of the enemy and the "distorted image" of our past life of sin must be removed in this hour as the image of Christ is fully formed in us.

Getting a **receipt**, according to the Dream Bible, *"represents standing proof of your choices being final.* **A reminder or evidence of what a choice you made in life cost you.** *Realization or remembering that your choice was final. Accepting or acknowledging some area of your life. Consider what the receipt is for additional meaning."*[xix]

In this dream some of the people did not receive a receipt because they have not made a choice to go all the way with Jesus. We must *receive* the Holy Spirit's presence and His fire into our lives in order to have all that is unholy burned up inside of us. Many have never "paid the price" so they have never received a "receipt" from the Lord showing them that they have gone through God's refining fire.

Jesus also showed me that many do not have the proper "Lighting" in their lives, for this "Light" comes only from the presence and the power of the Holy Spirit. Many desire to walk in the fullness of God's promises but refuse to surrender fully to Jesus and to allow His fire to refine them. Without repentance and this cleansing fire, they will never enter into the fullness that God has for them. If they continue to walk in their own strength and refuse the infilling of the Holy Spirit's power and anointing, they will have no power to walk on this "High Road of Holiness" and to receive this double portion anointing.

The Spirit of God showed me that there are many people who have denied His power and help so they are stumbling in *darkness* and cannot see where they are going. The Lord also told me that unless they repent, they will never get through the "security check line." The gate is narrow that He has called us to go through, and the road is hard, and few there are who find this path of glory. (See Matthew 7:14.) There is a "cost" in following Jesus all the way; it costs us everything that is hindering our relationship with Him, everything that we cling to apart from Him.

The Lord requires a full surrender of our will, our lives, if we are to enjoy the fulfillment of all that He has promised us, our "Promised Land." The Lord has so much to give us, but we can ignore His cry to draw close to Him and can lose out on His best gifts. What can compare to this glorious anointing that He so desires to pour into our lives in this new day? There are no riches or pleasures on this earth that can compare to the glory that He desires us to walk in. The Lord then gave me the following Scriptures that go along with my dream.

> So I advise you to buy gold from Me—gold that has been purified by fire. Then you will be rich. Also buy white garments from Me so you will not be shamed by your nakedness, and ointment for your eyes so you will be able to see.
>
> –Revelation 3:18 – NLT

> At midnight they were roused by the shout, "Look, the bridegroom is coming! Come out and meet him!" All the bridesmaids got up and prepared their lamps. Then the five foolish ones asked the others, "Please give us some of your oil because our lamps are going out." But the others replied, "We don't have enough for all of us. Go to a shop and buy some for yourselves." But while they were gone to buy oil, the bridegroom came. Then those who were ready went in with him to the marriage feast, and the door was

> locked. Later, when the other five bridesmaids returned, they stood outside, calling, "Lord! Lord! Open the door for us!" But he called back, "Believe me, I don't know you!"
> –Matthew 25:6–12

In these Scriptures we see the importance of being filled with the Holy Spirit and His power and that we cannot give to others what they are not willing to "buy" from the Lord. We can only come forth as "pure gold" if we go through the Spirit's refining fire. Every one of God's children must come to Jesus in order to be filled with the "oil" of the Spirit and His Light. We cannot give our "oil" to others, for they can only receive this infilling and anointing from the Spirit as they spend time with the Lord in the "secret place." Without the power of the Holy Spirit in this hour of darkness, we will never be able to walk as the overcomers that He has called us to be.

The **Dream Bible** can further your study on the symbolic meaning of these words: *receipt, bicycle, cake,* and *purse.* This site is a great help in interpreting our dreams, but the full meaning of them must always comes from the Holy Spirit. I have found that many times when the Spirit would show me the meaning of my dreams, it was nothing like I originally thought the dream was about. It will surprise you at times to find out the true meaning of your dreams!

> While being together and eating with them, He commanded them not to leave Jerusalem, but to wait for what the Father had promised, "Of which," He said, "you have heard Me speak. For John baptized with water, but you will be baptized and empowered and united with the Holy Spirit, not long from now."
> –Acts 1:4–5 – AMP

God's remnant has remained hidden until now, until this *season of glory.* They spent years with Jesus, eating and "dining" on His Word. They have been in a place of intercession and communion with their Savior for years, but now they have heard the voice of their Master telling them that it is time to move forward into the fullness that He has planned for their lives. They would not make a move apart from Jesus, but for years have been in training for this very time and season.

Jesus "commanded" them (His remnant) to wait in His presence until the day they would come out of their "wilderness" for their "appearing." (See Luke 1:80.) They have waited in God's presence in order to be prepared for their mission and to be fully empowered with the Holy Spirit's presence inside of them, for they knew that apart from the Spirit's power they would never be able to fulfill their calling. They are now united fully with the Spirit and can walk in the "greater works" that He has prepared for them to walk in. (See John 14:12.)

> When the day of Pentecost had come, they were all together in one place. And suddenly a noise like a violent rushing wind came from heaven, and it filled the whole house where they were sitting.
>
> –Acts 2:1–2 – NASB

The Church of the "Living Christ" is about to experience a **new** Pentecost, a fresh anointing, a double portion anointing from on High, and I believe that many of God's children have already received this anointing in order to overcome the darkness in this very generation. We are going to hear a "noise" as the Holy Spirit releases His power on this generation and as He comes with His "Mighty Wind" and blows afresh and anew on His people. It will look and feel "violent," at times, but it will lift God's true children up and into the *next glory* that He has prepared for them. The Lord's glorious presence will fill His "temple," His people, in a way that will bring everyone to their knees in adoration and in awe at what Jesus is doing in His true Church in this hour. Some of us have waited long for this glorious outpouring and this move of God's Spirit, and now we will see and experience what we have longed for!

Listen to the Father's voice saying:

> *"I have an 'upper room' experience planned for you, My faithful warriors. This is a new and a fresh encounter with the 'Living God.'*

*You have known My power, My anointing, in days gone by, but in this new season there is a **new** encounter with your God and an increase in the anointing that you have known in the past. This anointing will strengthen you internally and will rest upon you mightily. Many will see 'fire' resting upon you as you minister My word. This will be a new and a powerful experience for My called and chosen ones. The Holy Spirit already abides within you, but now you will be empowered in a measure that will overwhelm you.*

"*Get ready for this fresh and empowering experience in My Spirit. He will meet with you in your 'upper room,' that 'secret place' where you meet with Me daily. You will be embraced by Me in a way you have never known, and you will never be the same after these glorious encounters with My Spirit.*

"*Yesterday is gone, children. Look for Me now in new and exciting ways. I am not finished with you, with My Church, or with this world. Explosive, powerful displays of My glory and My power are here. They have arrived; look for them and do all that I ask of you, for I desire you to be a part of what I am doing in this very hour.*

"*No more excuses, for it is not about you, your own ability, wisdom, or power but about Me and what I can do in this dark world and in the wayward souls that are all around you. I am more than able to accomplish My will in this hour, but I need willing, obedient, and surrendered souls to work through, and I want you to be one of them. So, move forward. Delight in Me as I delight in you, and let no one take your 'crown,' your reward in Me, for it is full.*

"*So, listen, children, and listen carefully: 'In the next few weeks and months, you will have these new and powerful encounters with Me, and you must not shrink back from your calling and your destiny in Me.' Some of you have already encountered Me in this way, and you must lead and help others to embrace what I am doing in this hour. Tell them not to fear My presence but to draw close to Me, to embrace My fiery presence, My love, and to allow My Spirit to empty them and to purify them deeply with My Holy Fire. It is time to move forward, for the outpouring of glory has begun, and millions are already waking up to the late hour that they are living in.*

"I have set you apart, children, for My plan and My purpose. Resist Me no longer. Move with My Spirit and take 'new territories.' Take precious souls for Me; bring them to Me, and I will wash them; I will fill them, and I will flow through them in mighty ways. This is not the end. I am bringing in the final harvest quickly now. There is not much time left, children, for the time of harvesting will quit as quickly as it began. Trust Me; obey My voice and know that the very end of the ages is at hand!"

The Spirit of Unity

When they had entered the city, they went up to the upstairs room where they were staying, that is, Peter, John, James, and Andrew, Philip and Thomas, Bartholomew and Matthew, James the son of Alphaeus, Simon the Zealot, and Judas the son of James. All these were continually devoting themselves with one mind to prayer, along with the women, and Mary the mother of Jesus, and with His brothers .

–Acts 1:13–14

These Scriptures show us that Mary was with the disciples in the "upper room" *waiting* to be empowered by the Holy Spirit. She was in a place of *unity* with her brothers and sisters in Christ, a place of prayer and of obedience. This place of *unity* is where the Lord *commands the blessing and life forevermore.* (See Psalm 133:1–3.) This is the place the Lord is bringing His true Church to, and it is a place of power and of authority in His name. This oneness and unity in the Spirit will empower Christs' Church to walk together in sacrificial love and in a power that will cause this world to take notice.

For a long time the Church has looked too much like the world. The Church has been powerless and ineffective to make the changes that are necessary in this world, but all of this is changing in this new season. God's true children are rising up and are embracing each other as denominational walls are coming down. They are uniting their hearts in their mutual love for Jesus. Doctrinal differences will no longer divide God's people, for in these troubled times on the earth, the Lord's children are uniting in a way that this world has never seen before, and in this place of unity the Spirit is pouring out this powerful double portion anointing that we have waited and longed for.

> For when we place our faith in Christ Jesus, there is no benefit in being circumcised or being uncircumcised. What is important is faith expressing itself in love.
> –Galatians 5:6 – NLT

The Church will finally see that the most important thing is *faith expressing itself through Christ's love*. Faith must be shown through the loving acts of Jesus through our lives. I have seen and heard preachers and teachers teach on faith, but the message was devoid of love. Love is more important than the *gifts* we have been given, our ministry, or our position in the church. God's fiery love poured into us is what transforms our lives; this "fruit of the Spirit" must be the foundation that all the other "fruit" and gifts are built on. (See Galatians 5:22–23; 1 Corinthians 13:13.) Jesus wants to consume our lives with His love in this hour, and then all will know that we are true "disciples" of the Lord. As we are filled with the fullness of God's love, we will then have *faith to walk in the miraculous!*

> With all lowliness and gentleness, with longsuffering, bearing with one another in love, endeavoring to keep the unity of the Spirit in the bond of peace. There is one body and one Spirit, just as you were called in one hope of your calling; one Lord, one faith, one baptism; one God and Father of all, who is above all, and through all, and in you all.
> –Ephesians 4:2–6 – NKJV

Humility and gentleness will be the "hallmark" of God's end-time 11th hour workers. They will be patient with the wayward and be gentle with those who do not understand the ways of the Lord, for they will recall their own past struggles and will remember how kind and patient the Lord was with them. These are God's peacemakers who will do all that they can to keep unity in the Body of Christ. They know that there is only one Body, one Spirit, one Lord, one faith, one baptism, and one God and Father of all. We will see ourselves as the "family of God" and will care for one another in a way that will cause the heart of the Father to cry tears of joy.

> Therefore if there is any consolation in Christ, if any comfort of love, if any fellowship of the Spirit, if any affection and mercy, fulfill my joy by being like-minded, having the same love, being of one accord, of one mind. Let nothing be done through selfish ambition or conceit, but in lowliness of mind let each esteem others better than himself. Let each of you look out not only for his own interests, but also for the interests of others.
> –Philippians 2:1–4

The apostle Paul had the heart of the Father and a passion to see this unity lived out in God's children. His desire was to see God's love permeate the hearts of His people in a way that would eliminate selfish ambition and conceit. If we truly "esteemed others as better than ourselves," all-encompassng love would permeate the entire Church, and we would find this love flowing out to this lost and dying world, saving millions. This is what the Lord is after in this hour, and nothing will satisfy His heart more than this. God wants us to care for the needs of others as much as we care about our own needs, but this will only be realized as we are filled with the burning love of Jesus.

> Now I plead with you, brethren, by the name of our Lord Jesus Christ, that you all speak the same thing, and that there be no divisions among you, but that you

> be perfectly joined together in the same mind and in the same judgment.
>
> –1 Corinthians 1:10

As we develop the mind of Christ through daily meditation in His Word, we will then "speak the same thing" and there will be no divisions in the Church. If we refuse to line up with the Word of God and instead live by what **we** *feel* or *think* or by our **own** *natural reasoning,* how can we ever realize this glorious unity that our Father wants us to know? We need, as God's people, to understand more deeply the *ways* of our God, for truly, they are **not** our ways. Carnal, natural reasoning must be transformed fully through God's Word and the power of the Spirit. This is the time and the season to have the mind of Christ *fully* formed in us.

> We know that we have passed from death to life, because we love the brethren. He who does not love his brother abides in death. Whoever hates his brother is a murderer, and you know that no murderer has eternal life abiding in him. By this we know love, because He laid down His life for us. And we also ought to lay down our lives for the brethren. But whoever has this world's goods, and sees his brother in need, and shuts up his heart from him, how does the love of God abide in him? My little children, let us not love in word or in tongue, but in deed and in truth.
>
> –1 John 3:14–18

As I write this section I see how desperately I need this greater anointing and a deeper infilling of the Father's love. I believe many of God's people feel the same way. Only as we yield to the Spirit and receive this *greater anointing* and a *deeper love* for God's people will we experience the fullness of this *new day* that God is bringing us into. All bitterness and all resentment must be burned up in the fiery love of Jesus, and all of the deep internal wounds that we have suffered must be healed in His love.

Unforgiveness breeds hatred and pride, and we must never allow this to fester in our hearts. God sees **hatred** as *murder,* and we must realize the seriousness of allowing this root to remain in our hearts. If we desire to live eternally, this must be uprooted from our hearts and our lives, no matter what has been done against us. We must show our love by the deeds that we do as the Spirit leads us in Truth, not working according to our own standards or desires but walking in obedience to the Lord's will alone.

> The one who says, "I have come to know Him," and does not keep His commandments, is a liar, and the truth is not in him; but whoever follows His word, in him the love of God has truly been perfected. By this we know that we are in Him: the one who says that he remains in Him ought, himself also, walk just as He walked.
> –1 John 2:4–6 – NASB

So many of God's children want to walk in this greater anointing and to perform the "greater works" that He has promised in His Word, but they are not willing to keep His commandments or to follow His will for their lives. They are not obedient to the Father's will because they feel it is too hard and costly. They want the "easy road" of comfort and self-will, but the Lord will not anoint what man desires to do apart from His will. They say they "know" Jesus, but on that great Day Jesus will say: *"I never knew you."* (See Matthew 7:21–23.) Only those who truly follow His Word and who obey His commands will enter into eternal life. John tells us in the Word to walk just as Jesus walked. We can never do this in our own strength, but in the power of the Spirit all things are possible. How we need to be perfected in the love of the Father! This is His longing and desire for this very generation.

> Do not judge and criticize and condemn [others unfairly with an attitude of self-righteous superiority as though assuming the office of a judge], so that you will not be judged [unfairly]. For just as you [hypocritically] judge others [when you are sinful and unrepentant], so will you

be judged; and in accordance with your standard of measure [used to pass out judgment], judgment will be measured to you. Why do you look at the [insignificant] speck that is in your brother's eye, but do not notice and acknowledge the [egregious] log that is in your own eye? Or how can you say to your brother, "Let me get the speck out of your eye," when there is a log in your own eye? You hypocrite (play-actor, pretender), first get the log out of your own eye, and then you will see clearly to take the speck out of your brother's eye.

–Matthew 7:1–5 – AMP

Can you imagine what the Body of Christ would be like if there was no finger pointing or gossip? If instead of criticizing we would pray earnestly for those who are walking in error and in deception? There are times when we must confront others, but it must *always* be in love. I have, as a leader, had to confront others at times, but it was never something that I wanted to do in pride or in a "better-than-you" attitude. My heart never desires to hurt the person that I have to correct. I want to reveal Truth to them in a way that will *build them up* and will *help them to grow* to full maturity in Christ. When we truly believe that we have "not arrived," spiritually, we will then be able to confront others in deepest humility.

God despises self-righteousness, and all of us have failed in this area at times. Look how Jesus dealt with the Pharisees because they thought they were better than others. They judged many people wrongly, and because they would not deal with the "log" in their eye, they even ended up crucifying the Savior of the world. They even believed that Jesus worked miracles through the power of beelzebub. (See Matthew 12:24.) If we do not deal with the "log" in our own eye, we will never see clearly and be able to help others remove the "speck" in their eye. We do not want to stand before Jesus on Judgment Day and have Him tell us that we lived our lives on earth as a hypocrite or a pretender.

Those that are constantly judging others will never experience this greater and more powerful anointing that the Spirit is releasing; no "play actor" will know the fullness of joy that the Spirit is now releasing upon millions of souls. If we are truthful and honest about our own spiritual condition and about our failures, God can then give us a double portion anointing, and we will never judge anyone unfairly again. We will be gentle and will lovingly help them to see the "speck" that is in their eye.

> That they all may be one; just as You, Father, are in Me and I in You, that they also may be one in Us, so that the world may believe [without any doubt] that You sent Me. I have given to them the glory and honor which You have given Me, that they may be one, just as We are one; I in them and You in Me, that they may be perfected and completed into one, so that the world may know [without any doubt] that You sent Me, and [that You] have loved them, just as You have loved Me.
>
> –John 17:21–23

Can you feel the heartbeat of Jesus as you read these Scriptures? Can you feel how the Lord longs for this unity in the Body of Christ? Our King passionately longs to pour out this greater glory and anointing, but without this unity and oneness with Him and with each other this cannot happen. Jesus longs for this world to come to know His love, but if others don't see this powerful love of God pouring through our lives, they will only look at the Church and want nothing to do with us. Jesus longs to bring this great end-time harvest in, but first there must be a unifying love that will show this unbelieving world that Jesus is alive and well.

God's desire is to perfect us in His love, and this work will be completed in us through a fire that is heated "7 times hotter" than what we have known in the past. As His "Body" enters this *greater* fire that He has prepared, we will then be "melted" together as *one* in His love. Persecution and pain are the "tools" that our Father will use to bring His people together into this glorious oneness with Him and with each other. In the "furnace of affliction" we will become one with our Savior and will then be able to love those who differ from us. In God's love, as we become one with each other, the world will at last see who Jesus truly is and will run to Him and will surrender their lives fully to this glorious Savior. They will want to experience this love that they see in the Church, the true "Church of the Living Christ!"

> And now, little children, **abide in Him,** that when He appears, we may have confidence and not be ashamed before Him at His coming.
> –1 John 2:28 – NKJV, emphasis added

> Now he who keeps His commandments **abides in Him,** and He in him. And by this we know that He abides in us, by the Spirit whom He has given us.
> –1 John 3:24, emphasis added

> No one has seen God at any time. If we love one another, **God abides in us,** and His love has been perfected in us. By this we know that **we abide in Him, and He in us,** because He has given us of His Spirit. And we have seen and testify that the Father has sent the Son as Savior of the world. Whoever confesses that Jesus is the Son of God, **God abides in him,** and he in God. And we have known and believed the love that God has for us. God is love, and **he who abides in love abides in God,** and God in him. Love has been perfected among us in this: that we may have boldness in the day of judgment; because as He is, so are we in this world. There is no fear in love; but perfect love casts out fear, because fear involves torment. But he who fears has not been made perfect in love.
> –1 John 4:12–18, emphasis added

These Scriptures emphasize the importance of *abiding in Jesus* in order to know the depths of His love. His love alone is what perfects our lives and conforms us more fully into the image of Christ. God's love and presence is the greatest transforming power known on this earth. Apart from the love of Jesus we can never have the passion and the power, the anointing that will set us and others free from the powers of darkness. If we abide in Jesus and His Word abides in us, we will then bear much fruit, for apart from Him we can do nothing. (See John 15:4–8.)

We will never experience the faith that we need to walk in the miraculous unless we are filled with the presence of Jesus. If Jesus truly abides in us and we in Him, we will then know His *fullness* and a *joy* that this world can never give us. Only in this *union* with Jesus, being one with Him, will we be able to love others and love God as our hearts longs to. The Holy Spirit desires to perfect us in His love and to cast out all fear, for I believe that fear is what is keeping us from truly loving others as we should. We fear loss; we fear losing our place and our position in Jesus, and this all stems from deep insecurity and not having the fullness of God's love in our hearts. If we abide in God we will never suffer the "torments" of the enemy, for he will no longer have a foothold in our lives, and we will be free indeed!

We abide in God when we follow and keep His commands and do all that He asks of us. It is not grievous to obey the Lord but a delight and a joy to do His will. When we abide in Jesus we will then know His deepest passion and love for us and for others. Nothing could be greater than that! If we truly abide in the love of Jesus, we will have great confidence on that Day when we stand before Him. We will feel no grief or shame, for we have allowed His Spirit to fill us with the fullness of His love, and our hearts will know that we have loved others as He has loved us.

> One thing I have desired of the Lord, that will I seek: That I may dwell in the house of the Lord all the days of my life, to behold the beauty of the Lord, and to inquire in His temple.
>
> –Psalm 27:4

> When You said, "Seek My face," my heart said to You, "Your face, Lord I will seek."
>
> –Psalm 27:8

Some may be wondering: *But how can I receive this glorious fresh anointing from the Holy Spirit?* The Scriptures show us that they "waited" in the "upper room" in prayer and in expectancy, knowing that God would fulfill His promises to them. They were "focused" and seeking the Lord with their *whole* heart. They had one heart and one mind and that was to receive from the Lord the power of the Spirit that they so desperately needed and desired.

We need to be focused on seeking the Lord with our *whole* heart, fully surrendered to His will and to what He desires to impart into our lives in this hour. Jesus is telling us to seek His face above all and to remove the distractions that are keeping us from Him. This will require great diligence on our part. We will have to remove the "lesser things" in this world and make prayer and seeking the Lord our *highest priority.* Then, and only then, will we receive this glorious new and fresh anointing from on High, this double portion anointing that we need so desperately in order to fulfill our destiny and calling in Jesus. Only in this double portion anointing will the Body of Christ come to know and to experience *true* unity in the Spirit.

Hear the heart of Jesus:

> *"I am burning with deepest love for My children in this hour, and I am calling them to come closer to Me than they ever have. This is My heart; this is my deepest longing and desire. Tell My people to come close to Me so that I can 'burn' in their hearts and can remove what is hindering their relationship with Me.*
>
> *"They do not need more teaching but a desire to draw close to Me in prayer and in communion. They need to withdraw from earthly pleasures, come close to Me, and receive My fire, My burning love, so that no fear, no doubt, and no false idols will hinder them or take the place of My burning love. My people need Me, not 'platitudes,' not another 'formula' to know how to come to Me but an* **experience** *in My Spirit that will change their hearts and their lives forever.*
>
> *"Abiding in Me and Me abiding in them, spirit, soul, and body, is the answer. This is the answer to all of their 'dilemma's,' all of their confusion, and all of their anxiety. Nothing else will remove the fear from the hearts of My children except My LOVE. They need to know*

in their HEARTS that I love them. They need to EXPERIENCE Me in the depths of their being. Only this will free them internally: to truly know Me and to desire Me above all the things in this world.

"Tell them this: 'It is not so much head-knowledge as it is heart-knowledge...an experience in Me, My love, and My power so that they can truly walk in freedom and in the abundant life that I have for them.'

"Oh children, give Me 'space' in your life; come to Me and spend more time with Me, and you will encounter Me in new and glorious ways. I love you; I do not condemn you for your weaknesses and failures, for only in Me can you walk as an overcomer and come to know the fullness that I have for you. Come to Me! Come to Me and partake of Me: My Life, My Love, and My Power to overcome every obstacle that confronts you.

"I will not hurt you, but free you, and though it may bring some pain, know that in this spiritual 'surgery' you will experience a release of the Life you have so longed to live in Me. So come, come close and know that I will never give you more than you can bear. (See 1 Corinthians 10:13.) You can stand on this promise and believe it with your whole heart.

"I am for you, not against you. I love you too much to allow you to live in your sin, strongholds, and iniquities any longer. It is time for freedom. It is time for the fire of My love to consume you fully—says your God!"

Walking in Miracle Power

"I have entrusted you with great spiritual riches, and I know that I can trust you to use them for My glory and My honor. There is no greed or selfishness in you, My bride, but only a deep longing to give to others according to My will.

"And now for the next step, child, a step into the next glory, a greater glory and a greater power in order to enforce My will upon this earth. I will release through you My divine plan and My divine orders, and you will know that you are right in step with Me. You

have not looked to the right or to the left. You have not looked at what others are accomplishing for Me, but your eyes have focused on Me alone for direction in this hour, and I promise you: You will hear Me clearly and will see in the Spirit what I am doing.

"These are the last days, and I am releasing on My people a **greater anointing** in order to complete the 'greater works' that I have planned for this generation. You have not yet walked in the **fullness** of My end-time plans, but it will now be released to you as you spend time with Me in the 'secret place.' There is a fresh new 'blueprint' from Heaven that you will walk in, for now is the time of the greatest **display of glory** that this world has ever seen.

"Never have I loved you more, My children, and never have I longed so deeply to put your lives on 'display' for all the world to see. You will shine brightly, as I have spoken of in Isaiah 60, and you will know that you are My 'light' in a dark place. (See Isaiah 60:1–3.) The darker the world becomes, the more brightly you will shine for Me, and many will run into My Kingdom, for they will know that these are the last days.

"Glorious revelations are coming, and you will know things concerning My ways, the ways of My Spirit, in a deeper and a more profound way. You will teach the **way of the cross** clearly, and the **power of My resurrection** will flow through you to others. They will come out of their 'tombs' as Lazarus did, and they will do exploits in My name. This is the time and the season for this to be accomplished, and there is so much more to come!

"Prepare your hearts; prepare your lives, children, for what you have seen and have experienced in the past is nothing compared to what is ahead for you, My Church, your nation, and this world. Welcome the fiery trials, for they are purifying you deeply in this hour. These very trials are lifting you up to My throne of grace and are empowering you to walk in the miraculous. These very trials are releasing a stronger faith inside of you, even My faith, and in this faith, nothing will hold you back from accomplishing My whole will in and through your life. You have surrendered all, even your very life, and now you will receive My full reward for your obedience *and for the love you have shown to Me and to others. Look for this reward, for it is here. Receive what I have for you, for it is more glorious than you ever dreamed it would be—says your God!"*

> The Lord GӱԀԁ is my strength [my source of courage, my invincible army]; He has made my feet [steady and sure] like hinds' feet and makes me walk [forward with spiritual confidence] on my high places [of challenge and responsibility].
> –Habakkuk 3:19 – AMP

God has prepared and trained an army of Believer's to walk with Him in the High Place of power in this hour where signs, wonders, and miracles will be common-place. He has made their feet strong and steady, and they have been trained and conditioned through intense "warfare" to have confidence in their King and to move with the Spirit wherever He would lead them. They are fearless, and they have the "roar" of their King Jesus inside of them. Nothing will *move* this invincible army that the Spirit is raising up, for they have been anointed with a double portion anointing that will chase down devils and will destroy strongholds that many have said would never be removed. They have *faith for the miraculous* because they have been through the "fires of affliction" and have been made strong through countless trials and difficulties.

> God arms me with strength, and He makes my way perfect. He makes me as surefooted as a deer, enabling me to stand on mountain heights. He trains my hands for battle; He strengthens my arm to draw a bronze bow. You have given me Your shield of victory. Your right hand supports me; Your help has made me great. You have made a wide path for my feet to keep them from slipping. I chased my enemies and caught them; I did not stop until they were conquered. I struck them down so they could not get up; they fell

beneath my feet. You have armed me with strength for the battle; You have subdued my enemies under my feet. You placed my foot on their necks. I have destroyed all who hated me.
>
> –Psalm 18:32–40 – NLT

These warriors who have been trained by the Spirit will now walk in miracle power such as this world has never seen before. They have persevered and been strengthened in their trials, and now God has "qualified" them to walk with Him in the realm of the miraculous and to release miracles that will cause others to stand in awe and wonder.

Many will wonder where this group of passionate Believers have come from and why they have such power and ability in Christ. These have been the "hidden" ones who God is now raising up for all to see. They care not about fame or about receiving glory from man, but their passion is to see souls set free from the strongholds of the enemy and to do all that God requires of them, no matter the cost. Like Moses and John the Baptist, they have been trained in the wilderness but are now coming forth in the power and the anointing of the Holy Spirit.

> In the last day, that great day of the feast, Jesus stood and cried, saying, If any man thirst, let him come unto Me, and drink. He that believeth on Me, as the Scripture hath said, out of his belly shall flow rivers of living water.
>
> –John 7:37–38 – KJV

These warriors have been in the "secret place" with Jesus, drinking deeply of His love, and now "rivers of living water" are flowing from them. They are releasing God's power, authority, and miracle power into the earth, and millions of captives are now finding their freedom and liberty in Christ. This company of true Believer's continues to come to Jesus daily and to drink from Him, the "Fountain of Life" that never dries up. The Life of Jesus has now filled them, and they know that only in Him will strongholds be broken and the sick and the diseased be healed.

> To such an extent that they even carried their sick out into the streets and put them on cots and sleeping pads, so that when Peter came by at least his shadow might fall on one of them [with healing power].
>
> —Acts 5:15 – ASV

What we are *about* to see and are already *beginning* to see in this hour are miracles that this world has never seen! All true Believers who have been prepared for this hour, no matter their color, creed, or social standing in society, will now walk in a manner that will confound the Church. Many of God's children have walked in the tradition, teachings, and doctrines of men, but few have seen or experienced a *true move* of the Holy Spirit's power in their midst.

Those who are filled to overflowing will walk as the disciples of old, even in the miracle power that Peter and the Apostle Paul walked in. God is no respecter of persons, and what was done in the past will now come forth, I believe, in an even *greater* way and with a *stronger* anointing in *this* generation. We are the generation that will experience the "greater works" that Jesus promised we would walk in! (See John 14:12.)

> God gave Paul the power to perform unusual miracles. When handkerchiefs or aprons that had merely touched his skin were placed on sick people, they were healed of their diseases, and evil spirits were expelled.
>
> —Acts 19:11–12 – NLT

We will see *unusual* miracles in this hour, mind-boggling releases of power that will take our breath away! Words cannot express what we will see and will experience in this *decade of miracles and of power* that God has prepared for this very generation. Cancers will disappear; deaf ears will be unstopped and blinded eyes opened instantaneously. People that have been in wheelchairs for years, or even decades, will leap out of their wheelchairs and praise God for His mercy and His grace. We will see creative miracles, and limbs growing out where there were none, right before our eyes.

These miracles, and so many more, have happened in the past, but in this *decade of the miraculous,* they will come forth in a such a mighty way that multitudes will be healed and set free in a *moment,* even with no one laying hands on them. There will not be 1 or 2 miracles released in a church service, but hundreds and even thousands saved and delivered right before our eyes. Stadiums will be filled and outdoor services held where thousands will come and be blessed. I believe that what we will see in this generation will be overwhelming, for never has there been a time or a season like the one we have now entered into!

> I assure you and most solemnly say to you, anyone who believes in Me [as Savior] will also do the things that I do; and he will do even greater things than these [in extent and outreach], because I am going to the Father. And I will do whatever you ask in My name [as My representative], this I will do, so that the Father may be glorified and celebrated in the Son. If you ask Me anything in My name [as My representative], I will do it.
> –John 14:12–14 – AMP

What we have believed for, the promises that we have stood on for years will now come forth so quickly that it will make our heads spin. Jesus showed me years ago that those who have continued to trust and to believe in His promises through their dark circumstances will now experience *nonstop* blessings like a train that has endless boxcars filled with His glory and His gifts. This is God's glorious, end-time "glory train" filled with untold supernatural blessings that will be released upon His people in this very hour. This outpouring will be so great that God's people will find that every desire they have longed for will be given to them all because they have *believed* His promises and have *surrendered all* for the glory of His name.

> And I, brethren, when I came to you, did not come with excellence of speech or of wisdom declaring to you the testimony of God. For I determined not to know anything

among you except Jesus Christ and Him crucified. I was with you in weakness, in fear, and in much trembling. And my speech and my preaching were not with persuasive words of human wisdom, but in **demonstration of the Spirit and of power,** that your faith should not be in the wisdom of men but in the power of God.

–1 Corinthians 2:1–5 – NKJV, emphasis added

God will now flow through those who have surrendered their weakness and their brokenness to Him. They know that apart from His strength and His power they can do nothing. They lean hard on their Beloved Jesus and walk in the power of the Spirit to release all that He desires to do through their lives in this hour. These are the Lord's obedient ones who are weak in themselves but bold and strong in the Spirit. They know that they desperately need the power of the Spirit in order to release His anointing and His miracles so that others can be set free and healed of their sickness and their diseases. They know "nothing else but Jesus and Him crucified" (see 1 Corinthians 2:2) and that apart from Him nothing will be accomplished that is of any worth. (See John 15:4.)

These prepared ones know that what they preach and teach will have no effect apart from the Holy Spirit's anointing. These *surrendered ones* long for God's children to focus on Jesus alone and *His* love and His power, **not** on them or their own ability. They long for the Lord to show Himself strong to His people through His miraculous power, for this alone will awaken His people and will bring them home to His loving heart.

This is a **new day,** and there is a **new anointing** that is now coming down from an *open* Heaven, and all those who have open hearts will receive the fullness of this anointing and will go forth in **miracle power** and will set many who are bound free! Receive this anointing from on High and know that you have been set apart for "such a time as this!"

Listen to the heart of Jesus saying:

*"In this very year many will fall to their knees in deepest repentance and sorrow, for they will see that My heart of mercy is great. They will know at last that there is a **living** God who moves and*

who directs the nations as He desires. They will see that **I** control all things, **not** man.

"I have an army of true Believer's that are decreeing My Word, My Truth, and My Desires into the earth at this very moment. Unbeliever's, and even those who call themselves after My name but are not true Believers, will fall on their faces before Me in deepest repentance. Glorious revelations of who I am: My nature, My power, My glory, and My sustaining grace will now be released in an unprecedented measure. My glorious revelations of untold power and control will now be seen by **everyone** across the face of this earth.

"The news media will film incredible miracles, both in people and in nature. They will not be able to cover up the glorious manifestations of My love and My presence, for truly, it will be obvious to all. What you have seen in the past and are seeing now is only the very beginning of this great release of glory, this 'Great Awakening' that I have promised to My prophets and My servants. Now it will come to pass in a greater and stronger measure, and My true children will walk in this powerful move of My Spirit and set multitudes free.

"The first 'domino' has already fallen, and the **awakening** has begun, but I say: 'There is more to come, much more!' Keep your 'watch.' Pray with Me; decree My Word and My Truth through your anointed tongue and lips and marvel as you see Me move now in even greater power, showing this unbelieving world that I am alive and well.

"Look to the 'Mountain' and walk in the 'High Place' with Me, that place of faith and of power...that place where the impossible becomes possible. You will have faith to 'move mountains' now, faith for the miraculous, faith to see millions upon millions of souls saved and bodies healed. This is the time you have been waiting for, and there will be **no more delay.**

"Show yourself faithful to Me, and I will show Myself strong in your life; you will see glorious moves of My Spirit...things you never believed you would see on this earth. Glorious adventures await you; step into them now and begin to move with Me in a way that will shake not only souls to awaken them but will also shake and awaken cities and nations.

"This is the time of 'awakening,' and no tongue can tell, no tongue can express what I will do and what I am doing even now in your nation and the nations of this world. This is the season of glorious encounters with the living God. Come; feast with Me and partake of the new and glorious things that I have planned for your life. Doubt no longer; fear no more, for in this hour I am going to release My power, 'take back' nations, and bring many souls into My glorious Kingdom!"

Chapter 5

The Spirit and the Bride say: "Come!"

"The Spirit and the bride say: 'Come; come to the banquet table that I have prepared for you.' To all the hearts that have been made ready: 'Come, for you will partake of a feast more glorious, more sumptuous, and more delightful than any other earthly feast known to man.'

"Your 'garments' have been completed. They are 'white,' and you are covered and filled with My righteousness and My glory. All is prepared, and soon you will partake of this feast and will know the fullness of My love and joy. You have 'denied' yourself on this earth and have followed and obeyed Me; now you will have all that your heart has desired and so much more, more than you ever dreamed...things that have never entered your heart and mind. So come; all is prepared, and it is time for the 'celebration' to begin.

"I have called out to this generation to come to Me. Many have responded, and these very ones who have abandoned all for Me and surrendered their lives fully to do My will shall now taste of the glorious 'meal' that I have prepared for them. They have held nothing back but have stood on My promises through much 'fire' and persecution. They have been found worthy to walk with Me in 'white.'

"My precious bride, you have waited for this day; you have longed for this day, and many have responded to your cry to come home to My heart and to abandon all for Me and My Kingdom. And now your reward is in My hand—a greater reward than you could ever have dreamed or imagined. This reward will be known by you, not just now in smaller ways but in greater and more glorious ways throughout the eternal ages.

> "Many do not realize what they are giving up when they walk their own path and refuse to obey Me. There will be many tears on the Day of Judgment, for they will realize that they have 'forfeited' My best. They have settled for a 'meager crumb of joy' compared to the greater glory and honor they could have known in the 'Courts of Heaven.' Yes, they will know joy in their salvation, but they will realize on that Day that they could have had so much more—so much more glory and honor in the sight of all.
>
> "I will wipe away the tears from their eyes, for they will realize that they cannot go back and live their lives over again for Me. They can no longer pick up their cross and follow Me, and when they realize that it is too late to go back and win precious souls for Me, they will weep great tears of regret, but I will wipe their tears away and will reveal My heart of forgiveness to them.
>
> "Oh, children, you cannot realize what I have prepared for My obedient ones. Listen to the cries of My Spirit and My bride and come, for there is yet a very short span of time, and you can, even in this late hour, abandon all out of love for Me, and I will bless you in ways that will astound you—says your God!"

Can you hear Jesus calling you in this late hour? Can you hear His love call asking you to draw closer to Him than you ever have before? Jesus is calling you to come and to partake of the "feast" that He has prepared just for you…a *love feast* that will satisfy you fully and will fill you with His passionate love.

These have been days of preparation, and those who have followed the Lord fully in a walk of obedience and love are already clothed with a "white garment." Jesus already sees this *garment of glory* complete in Him. All is ready, and even now you can begin to taste of this glorious feast that Jesus is preparing for His bride.

Now is the time to give Jesus everything and to allow His Spirit to cleanse and to fill you full of His glory. This glorious season will not last long, for sooner than we think we will stand before Jesus and give an account of our lives. Only on this earthly plane can we pick up our cross, follow Jesus all the way, and release His will and His purposes on this earth.

Jesus does not want us to stand before Him empty-handed on that Day but to receive a full reward so that we can know the fullness of His joy. The Lord is calling us now, in this very hour, to come to Him, to run to Him, and to cry out to Him so that we can truly know Him in the depths of our being. Too many of God's children are content just going to Church and doing a few good works, but Jesus is calling us closer to Him than we have ever been in order to release His full Life in and through us to this generation. Hear His cry; come to the "banqueting table" and feast on His goodness, for He longs to satisfy your thirsty soul.

> "Come," says the Holy Spirit and the Bride in divine duet. Let everyone who hears this duet join them in saying, "Come." Let everyone gripped with spiritual thirst say, "Come." And let everyone who craves the gift of living water come and drink it freely. "Come."
>
> –Revelation 22:17 – TPT

The Spirit and the bride are crying out to all who will listen…to all who "have ears to hear"…to come to the "Water of Life" and to drink. Many have already responded, but there are yet multitudes that need to hear this glorious invitation from the King. This is an invitation to all who are broken and desperate for a touch from the Lord and are tired of the empty things of this world. Millions of souls are looking for freedom from their "chains" of sin and the strongholds that they feel they can never be free from. They have been looking for a way out of their "pit," and as they respond to the Spirit's invitation, they will be released from their "shackles" and be satisfied in the depths of their being. We will see many run to their Savior in this hour, and Jesus will not reject them no matter how deep their past sin and depravity has been. He will wash and cleanse them deeply and will release them from every "strangle-hold" of the enemy. This is the day and the hour when every "thirsty" soul who comes to Jesus will be fully satisfied, and they will never look to the world to meet their needs again!

> You there! Everyone who thirsts, come to the waters; and you who have no money come, buy and eat. Come, buy

> wine and milk without money and without cost. Why do you spend money for what is not bread, and your wages for what does not satisfy? Listen carefully to Me, and eat what is good, and delight yourself in abundance. Incline your ear and come to Me. Listen, that you may live; and I will make an everlasting covenant with you, according to the faithful mercies shown to David.
>
> —Isaiah 55:1–3 – NASB

So many in this world are trying to satisfy their deep hunger and thirst with the things of this earth, and this will never fill that *empty void* within their soul. There is only One who can satisfy the deepest recesses of the heart, and His name is Jesus. Many do not realize that they can "buy" the "wine" of His love for free if only they would come to Jesus, surrender their sin, and receive all that He has for them. Jesus is the "Bread" that came down from Heaven, and His food, His Word, presence, and love, is the *substance,* the Life, that truly satisfies the hungry and thirsty soul. Jesus is crying out to this generation to listen to the call of His bride and to come to Him. So many would rather do anything else, go anywhere else, but come to Him. He is calling out to this generation to make an everlasting covenant with Him through His cross and the blood that He shed for us all.

The Spirit and the bride are now one, and in unison they are crying out to this generation: *"COME...come and drink deeply from the 'Fountain of Life.'"* The "bride of Christ" is now walking hand-in-hand with Jesus in the power of the Spirit, and the love that pours from the bride will be an irresistible "magnet" drawing millions to Jesus. The bride will speak words of life to the multitudes, and the Spirit will draw them to Jesus, and at last their intense thirst will be satisfied. Nothing can compare with what we are about to see poured out on this generation as multitudes run to Jesus and at last realize that He alone can quench their deep thirst!

> Are you weary, carrying a heavy burden? Come to me. I will refresh your life, for I am your oasis. Simply join your life with mine. Learn my ways and you'll discover that I'm

gentle, humble, easy to please. You will find refreshment and rest in me. For all that I require of you will be pleasant and easy to bear.
—Matthew 11:28–30 – TPT

There is a time of great *refreshing* coming from the Spirit, but if we don't draw near to the Lord and come to Him when He is drawing us, how can we be refreshed and revitalized in His presence? God does not want us to fear Him but to respect and to honor Him. We must not allow *demonic fear* to keep us from His loving embrace. There is a reverential fear that God desires us to walk in, not a fear that will keep us at arm's length from Him. The Lord's desire is to lift every heavy "load" that His children are carrying, but His people must come to Him and join their lives with His Life, for only then will they know true freedom, peace, and joy on this earth.

The Spirit longs to release His refreshing Life and to reveal to all that Jesus is gentle, humble, and easy to please. As His people join Jesus through the Spirit, we will then know true rest and will realize that all of His ways are good and pleasant. When we try to go our own way apart from the Life of Jesus, the burdens of life will then overwhelm us. Jesus wants to refresh us, so let's run to our Beloved and spend time with Him in the "secret place," loving Him and allowing Him to fill us to overflowing with His love.

So be on your guard, not asleep like the others. Stay alert and be clearheaded.
—1 Thessalonians 5:6 – NLT

God is admonishing us to be on guard and to awaken fully to His call to come to Him, for only as we are filled with the Spirit daily will we stay alert and know the lateness of the hour. We must guard our hearts and minds so that we stay focused and alert concerning the hour that we live in. So many have fallen asleep, spiritually, but let this not be said of the Church; may she (The Church) hear Jesus' love call to come to Him and be satisfied and refreshed in His glorious presence.

Your King Jesus says:

"Hear My voice calling you this day to come to Me, to draw closer to Me than you ever have before. I have loved you with an everlasting love, but many of My children have refused to listen to My love call. They are busy doing many works and refuse to come to Me so that I can love them, speak to them, and fill them with My glory. I do not want My people to fear Me but to reverence Me and to love Me more than all the things of this world. I want to reveal to them My deep and passionate love, for this alone will free them to be all that I have created them to be.

*"Never have I loved you more, children, and My desire is to give you gifts and blessings that will overwhelm you, but you must come to Me and spend time with Me so that I can release in and upon you all the glory that I want you to receive. So look to Me alone in this hour and know that I love you with an everlasting love, a love so strong and so deep that it will overwhelm you in the days ahead. Hear My **love call** and come, come to Me and be set free spiritually, internally, physically, and in every area of your life. It is a **new day,** My people; do not look back but look forward to the **new things** that I have for your life.*

"Be at peace, for in the midst of all your trials, you will see Me in My glory, and I will dispel all of the darkness and lift you up to a higher plane in Me. I have so much for you in this hour...things that will take your breath away and will release you fully from your dark past. Look only to Me and listen only to My voice in this hour, for there will be many voices speaking, trying to distract you from your unique calling and destiny in Me. This is why you must spend time with Me, listening to My voice and allowing My Spirit to lift you up and into the next glory that I have prepared for you.

"Come to Me; come to Me and be blessed exceedingly, abundantly, above and beyond all that you could ever ask or imagine. (See Ephesians 3:20.) I have so much to release in and through your life to this generation. 'For such a time as this' I have set you in this very generation to do all that I ask of you, for there are new things that I will require

*you to do, new places that I will ask you to go, and a greater power that I will now release through your life. The time is now, and this is the **decade of glory** that I have placed you in. You are not a mistake; you are not just a casualty of fate but My called 'messenger' who will release the Good News of My salvation to many, many souls in this very hour. Trust Me now and move forward into all that I have for you: the 'good works' that I have planned for you to walk in even before the foundation of this world—says your God!"*

The Fullness of Time – No More Delay!

Hear what the Lord is saying:

*"When I come as a 'Blazing Fire' and a 'Refreshing Wind,' know that the time is short, children. It's time to let go fully of everything that is **binding** you. I want you to be fully prepared and readied to enter My 'Banquet Hall.' You must be dressed in 'white,' in 'fine linen,' in order to partake of this glorious feast. No one defiled, no one that is holding onto darkness or the things of this world will taste of this feast. Only those fully prepared will come and dine with the mighty King, the Bridegroom.*

"I have called and called. I have drawn you with strong 'cords of love'; resist Me no longer. Run to Me and allow My Spirit to remove the 'rags' you have been wearing for so long. I have new and glorious things prepared for you, but you must surrender the deepest part of your heart to Me.

"I speak this in deepest love and also as a warning, for I am not a God to be 'trifled' with. Remember My Word, children: 'Do not be deceived, God is not mocked; for whatever a man sows, that he will also reap' (Galatians 6:7 – NKJV). Do you think I will overlook what you have hidden deep in your soul? Do you think that I will wink at the 'dark secrets' that are hidden in your heart? This is the time of uncovering, and everyone, no matter who he or she is, who refuses this uncovering, this time of confession and cleansing of sin, I say: 'It will be too late to ride the high "wave of glory" that is coming with Me.'

"Run to Me, children; 'undress' before Me, spiritually; take off your 'spiritual mask' and allow My fire to penetrate that deep place within you. These are My last warnings, My last callings, and all who respond to My words, to My love, and to My dire warnings will be saved in this hour, and My Spirit will do a quick and mighty work in their lives and make all things new.

"No more 'playing church!' No more playing with the things of this world! No more sitting on the 'fence of compromise!' You are either for Me or against Me. Know that I am for you, and I do not desire to see even one soul perish. This is not My heart, this is not My desire, not for you or for any other soul that I love so deeply. Do not ignore My cries any longer! Do not believe that this word is for everyone else but you! Look in the mirror and say: 'I am the one who needs to repent. I am the one who needs to be purified and cleansed in this hour.' If you will do this…if you will be honest with Me, I promise you, I will uncover your soul and show you the deep, hidden iniquities that you have feared to look at and have refused to deal with. I am a merciful and loving God; so, come; run to Me, and you will know My mercy and love. I will not destroy you. I will not bring undue pain and grief; I will only bring what is necessary for your spiritual health so that you can enjoy full freedom and liberty in My Spirit—says your God!"

He answered, "The Father is the one who sets the fixed dates and the times of their fulfillment. You are not permitted to know the timing of all that He has prepared by His own authority."

–Acts 1:7 – TPT

The Father is the One who sets the fixed dates and times for their fulfillment, and no one can change these times, these "fixed dates." There is always a "fullness of time" on God's calendar, an opportune time when conditions are right. During this *opportune time* we will see the Lord move in might and power. I believe with all of my heart that we have entered a

"Kairos" time when we will see the hand of God move in extraordinary ways to fulfill on this earth His will and purpose in our midst! According to *Merriam-Webster Dictionary*, **Kairos** time is: *"a time when conditions are right for the accomplishment of a crucial action: the opportune and decisive moment."*[xx]

> But when the fulness of the time came, God sent forth his Son, born of a woman, born under the law.
> –Galatians 4:4 – ASV

As I was preparing this section in my book, so many Scriptures in the Bible came alive to me. Scriptures that I had read *many* times before suddenly burned in my heart as I felt the Spirit confirm to me that there would be *no more delay* and that the *fullness of time* has arrived! My spirit has been "stirred" by the Spirit of God for some time now, and I know others have also been sensing the same things that God is showing me. The Lord does not want us to be anxious but alert concerning the late hour that we live in. He wants His Church fully "awake" and *ready* to move with Him when He calls.

Saints of God, we do not have much time left to get our "house in order." The Lord has spoken to me and has told me to warn as many people as possible about what is coming to the earth...to empty our hearts and our lives of the things of this world so that the Spirit can fill us full of His presence. Jesus is calling; the Spirit and the bride are crying out and saying: *"Come,"* and we must have "ears to hear" what the Spirit is saying *right now*, in this very generation.

So many cannot hear what the Lord is saying because they have heard these warnings many times before. They just ignore the cries of the Spirit, but I believe that in this great "shaking" that is around the corner millions will at last be awakened to the soon coming of Jesus. Some will continue to follow their own path and to do their own will, but they will never be able to say that God did not warn them.

Day after day the Spirit is speaking to me about what is about to "explode" upon the earth! I've been having many dreams about this *great awakening* and about the *final harvest* that He desires to bring in. So many believe that there is yet much time before the coming of the Lord, and they do not feel a *sense of urgency* in their spirit-man, but I do. And I know that others do as well. In many of my dreams lately God is showing me that this is the time when we will be fully delivered from our past and freed completely from fear and unbelief. God's desire is that we walk in the *full* freedom of His Spirit. He has been calling and crying out to many hearts in this hour, but few have truly been listening to His voice.

So many are talking about the *uncovering* in our nation and in other parts of the world, but God is desiring to uncover what is in **our** hearts in this hour. His desire is to purify us in the depths of our being in order to flow through us and so that we can *ride* this coming "Wave of Glory" with Him. Every hindrance must be removed if the Spirit is to have free reign in our lives. There is a greater "Light" coming from the Spirit, and what is hidden deep in our hearts will be exposed.

In a recent dream God confirmed to me that this uncovering is coming through this greater "Light," the Light of the Holy Spirit. In this dream I was in my bedroom, and when I woke up I could see a huge "cobweb" that I had never seen before. I tore this web down and then walked into the hallway of my house where I saw a **huge spider** on the wall and captured it. I felt the strength of this spider as I held it down and cried out for the Lord to come and "finish it off." The Lord came and took the spider so He could flush it down the toilet!

The Lord showed me that when this brighter "Light" comes His people will see things in their hearts that they have never seen before. It's the same way in the natural: When a room is dimly lit, you see little of the dust and dirt that is around, but if someone comes with a bright light, all at once you see every little piece of dirt and even dust floating in the air! In the same way our God is coming with a bright "Light" in this hour in order to free us completely so that we can walk in the High Place with Him. The Spirit wants to flow through us unhindered, but without this deeper work being accomplished in our hearts and lives, we will just continue to go on our merry way and believe that we have all the time in the world to deal with these "deeper issues" in our lives.

> Behold, I (Jesus) am coming quickly, and My reward is with Me, to give to each one according to the merit of his

deeds (earthly works, faithfulness). I am the Alpha and the Omega, the First and the Last, the Beginning and the End [the Eternal One].
–Revelation 22:12–13 – AMP

Jesus is coming to reward His faithful children, even now, on this earthly plane. This reward will lift His "elect" up to higher ground where they will walk with Jesus in miracle power. Jesus has called them, and they have responded with their "yes." They have heard the cry of the Spirit deep in their hearts and have obeyed the Father's will daily in their close and intimate walk with Him. This is not just for a select few but for the entire Church. Yet few have truly responded to the cry of His heart. This is a sad statement, but I believe that in the days ahead this will change drastically as the Lord makes Himself known to His people in judgment and in His glory. His fire will awaken many "sleepy" souls as His passionate love fills them full.

Do this, knowing the time, that it is already the hour for you to awaken from sleep; for now salvation is nearer to us than when we first believed.
–Romans 13:11 – NASB

The Spirit keeps speaking to my heart that Jesus is coming sooner than what most of His people believe. In this *new day* and *great awakening*, many will be awakened out of their slumber. Because of these past years of delay in not seeing the fulfillment of the Lord's promises and the many trials and temptations His people have gone through, many of God's children have lost hope and are no longer pressing into the heart of Jesus. But the fire of God that is coming will awaken many souls, and they will have a renewed passion and desire for Jesus. Millions in the Church will return to their "first love," Jesus, and they will spend hours in the "secret place" with Him in prayer and in worship. Thousands upon thousands will be set free and healed of chronic illnesses as the Spirit moves in unprecedented ways in this generation.

Then the word of the LORD came to me, saying, "Son of man, what is this proverb that you have in the land of Israel, saying, *'The days are long and every vision fails'?* Therefore tell them, 'Thus says the Lord GOD, "I will put an end to this proverb, and they will no longer use it as a proverb in Israel." But say to them, "The days draw near as well as the fulfillment of every vision. *For there will no longer be any false and empty vision or flattering divination within the house of Israel.* For I the LORD will speak, and whatever word I speak will be accomplished. *It will no longer be delayed,* for in your days, O rebellious house, I will speak the word and I will fulfill it," says the Lord GOD.'" Again the word of the LORD came to me, saying, "Son of man, behold, the house of Israel is saying, 'The vision that Ezekiel sees is for many years from now, and he prophesies of the times that are far off.' Therefore say to them, 'Thus says the Lord GOD, *"None of My words will be delayed any longer. Whatever word I speak will be fulfilled completely,"'"* says the Lord God.

   –Ezekiel 12:21–28 – AMP, emphasis added

These Scriptures in Ezekiel "jumped off the page" as I read them recently, and I knew that God was speaking to my heart concerning this very generation. So many have closed their ears to the words of the prophets, but they are now beginning to hear what the Spirit is saying because of the "shakings" that are occurring on the earth. There have been many false prophets speaking words from the soulish realm and from their own "imagination," but I believe that God has *true* prophets in this hour who are hearing the voice of the Spirit clearly.

The Spirit is dealing with false prophets and "empty visions" in this hour. We are entering a time when the Lord will no longer tolerate false teachings and false prophets in His Church. This is a serious hour, and God is about to "judge" His people *for it is time for judgment to begin in the house of the Lord.* (See 1 Peter 4:17a.) God is going to speak and is already speaking through His true prophets, and what they speak will come to pass quickly. God is confirming in this hour what He has spoken through them and what the Spirit will speak in the days ahead. I do not believe that we will have to wait years to see the fulfillment of what the Spirit is saying to this generation, but suddenly, quickly, we will see these prophecies come to pass.

There will be no more delay, for this is the time, the *decade of glory*, when we will not only see our personal promises from God come to pass but will see the many prophecies concerning our nation and this world come to pass as well. Our time of waiting is over, and we are about to see dreams, promises, and visions that have been spoken to us years ago come to pass as "flashes of lightning!" One after another we will receive all that the Lord has promised us, for ourselves, our families, and this entire earth. This is God's time; it is His *appointed time*, and soon this whole earth will see that our God is alive and well!

> Then the children of Judah came to Joshua in Gilgal. And Caleb the son of Jephunneh the Kenizzite said to him: "You know the word which the Lord said to Moses the man of God concerning you and me in Kadesh Barnea. I was forty years old when Moses the servant of the Lord sent me from Kadesh Barnea to spy out the land, and I brought back word to him as it was in my heart. Nevertheless my brethren who went up with me made the heart of the people melt, but I wholly followed the Lord my God. So Moses swore on that day, saying, 'Surely the land where your foot has trodden shall be your inheritance and your children's forever, because you have wholly followed the Lord my God.' And now, behold, the Lord has kept me alive, as He said, these ***forty-five years***, ever since the Lord spoke this word to Moses while Israel wandered in the wilderness; and now, here I am this day, ***eighty-five years old***. As yet I am as strong this day as on the day that Moses sent me; just as my strength was then, so now is my strength for war, both for going out and for coming in. Now therefore, ***give me this mountain of which the***

Lord spoke in that day; for you heard in that day how the Anakim were there, and that the cities were great and fortified. It may be that the Lord will be with me, and I shall be able to drive them out as the Lord said." And Joshua blessed him, and gave Hebron to Caleb the son of Jephunneh as an inheritance. Hebron therefore became the inheritance of Caleb the son of Jephunneh the Kenizzite to this day, because he wholly followed the Lord God of Israel.

–Joshua 14:6–14 – NKJV, emphasis added

The Lord reminded me recently about Caleb and how he faithfully continued to stand on the promises of God for **45 years**. Only Caleb and Joshua believed God's promises concerning the Promised Land, and they alone, out of those who spied out the Land, trusted the Lord to fulfill His promises to them that He would conquer all of the "giants" and bring them into the "Good Land." All the other spies gave a negative, fearful report concerning what they had encountered as they spied out the land, and so all of Israel, even the faithful children of God, had to wander in the desert for 40 years. (See Numbers 13:1–14:38.)

There are some who are reading this that have waited many, many years for their promises from God to come to fruition. Jesus reminded me that I have been one who has waited 45 years to see the fulfillment of all the promises He has made to me throughout my life. Jesus told me that now is the time for these promises to be embraced and enjoyed.

Some of these *seniors* believe that their time of "fruitfulness" is over, but it is not. This is a time of renewal and of strengthening from the Spirit of God so that we can take back from the enemy all that he has stolen from us. It is a time when we will walk in the inheritance that we have fought for, waited for, and believed for. It is the time, the *new day*, that we have waited for, and now we will realize fully that we have not waited in vain.

Even as Caleb waited and was faithful through his wilderness journey so have God's company of "seasoned warriors," and they will now go forth and take the "Land." Caleb took that "mountain" where "giants," the Anakim, were living in fortified cites. It doesn't matter how impossible your situation looks, you <u>can</u> take your "mountain" in the power and the strength of the Spirit. If you stand on your promises from God as Caleb did, your God will come through for you no matter how long it takes, and you will take the inheritance that the Lord has promised you. You <u>will</u> be delivered from the enemy and will plant on top of your *mountain* a "flag of victory!" Remember: Your faith and trust in Jesus and His covenant promises *always* wins!

What God has promised me and promised you will now be given to us because we have followed the Lord wholeheartedly, just as Caleb did. We have walked in faith and in trust, and now Jesus is releasing the reward that He has for every warrior who has stood in faith and not backed down when the enemy came against them in rage. We have believed that God would fulfill every promise that He has spoken to us. We are the Lord's end-time Caleb's who will now come forth in power and be an example of faith and trust in a Savior who has never failed us. Let's go forth now and take our "mountain," our inheritance in Christ! I pray that this prophetic word will bless you greatly.

Receive this encouraging word from the Lord:

> *"You are My Caleb, and it is time to take that 'mountain.' Be not afraid neither be dismayed because of the long delay. You have waited and waited; you have trusted and surrendered your life to Me and followed Me* **wholeheartedly,** *and now My reward, your inheritance, is being released to you. I am giving you this 'mountain,' and you will bring down every 'giant' in your life, not only for yourself but for many, many souls that have been held captive by these 'giants.'*
>
> *"Take this 'mountain'; it is yours. Do not back down, but in My Name conquer every 'giant' that has tried to stop you from moving forward into the fullness of your inheritance. It's time to move forward, children. Be not dismayed because of the long delay that you have known, for now every 'shackle' will break and your feet will no longer be 'fettered.' It is time. Take this 'mountain' that has stood before you for so many years. I have heard your cries and seen your tears these many years, and I have not forgotten the promises that I made to*

you. I will renew your strength, and you will 'mount up with wings as an eagle' and soar with Me now, for I will fulfill every promise that I have made; there will be no more delay. (See Isaiah 40:31.)

"You have been found faithful. You have wholeheartedly followed Me, and it is time for you to receive all that I have promised you. Every promise will now be fulfilled, and you will walk with Me on My 'Mountain of Glory' and sing praises to Me. You will shout your victory in Me, and all will hear of what I have done for you in fulfilling every promise I have made to you.

"Yes, you are My called and faithful one; the one I will honor in the sight of all because you have stood on My promises and not backed down in the face of all the lies of the enemy and his tormenting attacks. You have remained faithful and stood strong, and now I will renew your strength and will remove years of weariness because of your fierce battles. I will 'renew your youth' as I have promised in My Word, and all will stand amazed at your undaunting spirit and courageous stand against all the darkness that has come against you. (See Psalm 103:5.) You will give Me all the honor, glory, and praise, and you will stand strong and complete the mission that I have given you with joy, praise, and a delight in Me that you have never experienced.

"Your reward is here; take it...take the fullness I have for you, for I am your exceeding, great reward." (See Genesis 15:1.)

> He made known to us the mystery of His will according to His good pleasure, which He purposed in Christ, with regard to the fulfillment of the times [that is, the end of history, the climax of the ages]—to bring all things together in Christ, [both] things in the heavens and things on the earth.
>
> –Ephesians 1:9–10 – AMP

I believe we have entered the "climax of the ages," and what we are about to experience will validate what this Scripture says, for our God is bringing "all things together in Christ." We will see a "uniting" of the things that are in Heaven with the earth through many miracles, signs, and wonders that the Lord will release upon this generation. God's people will know that they are "seated with Christ in heavenly places." (See Ephesians 2:6.) They will know a *oneness* with the Spirit that no other generation has experienced…a power flowing through them that will astound this world. Because God's remnant has responded to the Spirit's "Come" and have quenched their "thirst" with His "Living Water," they are now filled to overflowing and walk in miracle power and the glory of their King, Jesus.

In a recent dream I saw a great *flood of water*, and there were many people in these waters. I knew this flood was dangerous, and I felt that some of the people in this flood would not make it. This flood came all the way up to my parent's house, and I was concerned about the safety of my family. *Annie*, my sister, had made it safely through the flood, and I was told that she was at a *restaurant eating.* Some of the people that made it through the flood had some kind of *breathing apparatus* on their face. At first, I thought that they were *pacifiers*, but they showed me this *device* and told me that it helped them *breathe under water.*

In another part of my dream, I was in a large building, and there was a *sense in the atmosphere* that something big was about to happen. As I looked around I saw a group of *very strong looking horses.* There was a feeling of *great power* coming from them. They looked fearsome! They started to ascend some steps and *gathered together.* It seemed as if they were "wired up" and waiting to be released. There was a great sense of expectancy, awe, and wonder all around them! I started going up the steps near them, and someone warned me to walk quietly past them because they didn't want me to "stir up" the horses. I then started to enter a *large hall* where other people had gathered, and as I looked at the horses, a small foal tried to enter this hall, but another horse stopped this young horse from going in.

Jesus showed me that a *great flood* is coming, a flood of mercy and grace and also of judgment, and many will find themselves in *deep water. Annie* represented those who have a personal relationship with Jesus in prayer and in obedience. They will be safe and will be found "dining" with the Lord (she was in the restaurant). Those with *pacifiers*, those who are clinging to this world and refuse to *grow up* in Jesus, will also find themselves in deep water, and they will cry out to Jesus to rescue them in the days ahead. Then there are those who know the *depths* of the love of God. They know how to "breathe" underwater. They are filled with the life of Christ, the "water" of the Spirit, and they know how to swim in the *deep waters* of His love. They have learned to walk in the Spirit and to live in Him through every *flood* and every trial they have gone through.

It was my sister *Annie* who was eating in the restaurant, and the name Annie is "a variant of Anna which is the Hebrew name Hannah, meaning 'gracious' or 'favored' or 'merciful.'"[xxi] In Hebrew the meaning of the name Annie is prayer.[xxii]

I have had several dreams about God's end-time *horses*, and He has shown me many things concerning how He will flow through them in this final hour. Jesus told me that the *horses* in my dream *symbolize* His end-time remnant who have gathered together and are ready to "break loose," run with Him into the harvest field, gather precious souls, and set many captives free. These *horses* are filled with expectancy and ready to move with the Spirit at a moment's notice. They are filled with the power of the Spirit and are following their King alone. They are focused and not distracted by the things of this world. This is the Lord's bride, and no one will stop them. They are being released in this very hour to do the bidding of the Lord.

Horses symbolize war, courage, power, wisdom, and glory.[xxiii] They also symbolize force, strength, and the status of a King or Country. [xxiii] These are God's *anointed ones* who have been set aside for this time, this new era, and they will now be released in God's power and glory. They will not be moved by any evil force that comes against them, for they have been spiritually *conditioned* and *positioned* by the Lord.

The Spirit of God showed me that there will be *no more delay*. God's people have gathered together (in the dream I gathered with others in a large hall), and they are even now "feasting" in Jesus' "Banquet Hall" and enjoying intimate communion with Him. All is in order, divine order, and our God is having His way in this generation for He has found a faithful few who will follow Him all the way and who will accomplish His end-time purposes.

The **"Horse Gate"** was the 8th gate of Jerusalem in Nehemiah's day.[xxiv] It's next to the East Gate.[xxiv] We know that one of the meanings for the number 8 is "new beginnings."[xxv]

We have entered an era of *new beginnings* in our lives, our nation, and in this world. It is not the *fullness* of what God has in store, but it will be a glorious beginning of what our God can and will do in exposing evil, proclaiming righteous judgments, releasing His glory, saving a multitude of souls, and turning many things around for our good and for His glory.

> Have you given the horse strength or clothed his neck with a quivering mane? Have you made him able to leap forward like a locust? His majestic snorting is something to hear! He paws the earth and rejoices in his strength, and when he goes to war, he is unafraid and does not run away though the arrows rattle against him, or the flashing spear and javelin. Fiercely he paws the ground and rushes forward into battle when the trumpet blows. At the sound of the bugle he shouts, "Aha!" He smells the battle when far away. He rejoices at the shouts of battle and the roar of the captain's commands.
> –Job 39:19–25 – TLB

This perfectly describes God's end-time army, His "horses," that will run with Him in this final hour, tear down the "gates of hell," and set many captives free from the "chains" of the enemy. His *horses* are spiritually *aggressive* and will not back down no matter how fierce the battle that rages against them. These *horses* have no fear, and if you have ever seen the movie "War Horse," I believe that the horse in this movie shows a powerful picture of God's end-time *war horses* and of His bride that wears "combat boots!" There are so many spiritual parallels in this movie, and I encourage you to watch it.

The "bride of Christ" has great spiritual discernment, and she hears the voice of her Master clearly. She goes where He wants her to go and speaks His "words of fire." This "war horse" runs toward every giant and will never back down in the face of fear! These are God's end-time *horses* that will move "mountains" out of the way that stand before God's children, and they will lift up His people to know who they truly are in Christ. They have heard the Spirit's cry; they have quenched their "thirst," and these passionate warriors are now ready to "take the Land!"

> And now my head will be lifted up above my enemies around me, in His tent I will offer sacrifices with shouts of joy; I will sing, yes, I will sing praises to the LORD.
> –Psalm 27:6 – AMP

The Lord gave me Psalm 27 in another recent dream, and again, God was confirming to me that there will be no more delay in releasing His plans and His purposes in our generation. In this dream He personally showed me that my time of struggle and testing was over and that I would now rejoice in the *full* victory that He was giving me over *all* of my enemies. There would now be a manifestation in my life of not only total freedom and joy in Him but an enjoyment of wholeness: spirit, soul, and body that I would now walk in. What has been delayed in my life will now come forth in the fullness of the Spirit.

I believe that this revelation in Psalm 27 was not only for me but for all who have stood on His promises and believed for total healing in areas of their lives where they feel they have been "stuck" for a long time. This is the day of freedom and of victory for all who have believed that God would fulfill every promise that He has spoken to them.

> And will not [our just] God defend and avenge His elect [His chosen ones] who cry out to Him day and night? Will He delay [in providing justice] on their behalf?
> –Luke 18:7

God has heard our cries and is moving on our behalf in new, glorious, and exciting ways. The time is now, and the delay is over! Release is coming to millions of captives! The *last chapter* of His "Book" is now being released, and it will be glorious. Most of the time the last chapter in a book is the most intense, wonderful, and victorious one, and do you think that God's *book* for our lives, this nation, and the world will be any less exciting and breathtaking? I believe this last chapter that Jesus is writing will release awesome turnarounds in our lives and in the nations of this world as we experience this Great Awakening. The Lord's end-time plans will cause us to stand in awe and in wonder, and we will praise our King from the depths of our being as He releases His glory and His power on this very generation that He has prepared to receive it.

> FOR YET IN A VERY LITTLE WHILE, HE WHO IS COMING WILL COME, AND WILL NOT DELAY.
> –Hebrews 10:37

> Declaring the end and the result from the beginning, and from ancient times the things which have not [yet] been done, saying, "My purpose will be established, and I will do all that pleases Me and fulfills My purpose."
> –Isaiah 46:10

God's salvation is near; it is here even this day; just reach up and cry out to Jesus, and He will meet with you. The Father's purpose will be established, and He will do all that pleases Him! Our God is Almighty, and no devil will thwart His plans and His purposes for this generation. All will come to pass according to His will and His desire for this nation and this world! Jesus has already seen the end of all things, not only for this world but for our personal lives; He never fails to complete the work that He has begun in our lives. (See Philippians 1:6.)

He will satisfy your deepest longing for His love and His presence; only come to Jesus and receive all that He has for you. Look diligently for His glorious power to manifest in your life and free you from every torment and affliction that has weighed you down. I promise you: As you surrender all to Jesus, you will find His freedom and all that your heart longs for; Jesus will NOT fail you! Respond to His cry, to His invitation to come to Him and to drink deeply of His love, and He will meet with you in the most extraordinary ways. Jesus loves you, and it is time for you to come home to His heart!

To every thirsty soul Jesus says:

> *"For those of you who have truly repented and followed me in obedience, I say to you: 'The time of delay is over. Your time of struggle and of barrenness, spiritually, is over! You have waited for Me, and you have not waited in vain. Look to the sky; look to the clouds, for now you will see My glory descend upon you, the nations, and this world.'*
>
> *"Some will actually see a visible 'cloud of glory' over their lives and over others. They will see cities and even nations covered with this 'cloud of glory.' Your eyes will now see what your heart has believed for! Many will see angels in this hour, not only those that are around them but millions of angels moving through cities and nations, wielding fiery swords and doing battles in the heavenlies. Some of you reading this word will see astounding things in the supernatural realm. Though your spiritual eyes have been blinded for a season, now the 'blinders' will be removed, and you will see into the Spirit-realm in a measure you never have before.*
>
> *"This is the time you have waited for, longed for, and have all but given up on ever seeing! Some of you have waited on the sidelines for so long that you have fallen asleep and no longer believe that what I have promised you will come to pass. Now you will see; now you will experience My glory in a way you never dreamed you would. You are about to receive a 'shock treatment,' and you will come alive to all that I have promised you, and you will walk in those promises! 'Hope deferred' has made your heart sick, and you have been 'slack,' spiritually, because of this. You have grown weary in the waiting, but I am about to breathe on you and* **resurrect** *you in a way you have never experienced before. You will feel My Life flowing through you in power and in strength, and you will fully embrace My call and My destiny for your life. Don't look to man to accomplish this in your life; look only to Me, for I alone will accomplish this work in and through you.*

*"You have wondered if your season of loss and of suffering would ever end, but I say to you this day: 'It is over; it is finished, and now you will see Me move in unprecedented ways.' I will place 'spiritual paddles' on your heart and bring you back to 'life.' All that is **dead** in your life will be forever gone. New life is now entering into you; receive it; believe it, for the time has come for you to move with My Spirit into your city, your nation, and the nations of this world. You will move with Me in new strength and power, and you will never again feel the weariness that you have experienced in the past. All will be washed away in My glory and My power. This work will be accomplished quickly now, and you will know that you have not waited for Me in vain."*

God's End-Time Revelations through Dreams and Visions

"In this Great Awakening, this glorious new era, there will be a resurgence of dreams and visions. There will be powerful visitations coming upon My people through the appearances of angels giving instruction and help to those in need. I will visit My people in their dreams and give them wisdom and direction for their lives, and I will confirm what I have spoken in the Book of Joel. (See Joel 2:28–29.)

"These divine 'occurrences' will come frequently and in rapid succession, and all will know that My coming is imminent. What you have experienced in the past, children, is nothing compared to the outpouring of My Spirit in this hour. These outpourings will change not only individual lives but also cities and nations in the near future.

"Kings will come to you, leaders of nations, and ask for your advice. They will ask for wisdom and discernment concerning the dreams and visitations that they are receiving from Me. It will be much like Pharaoh asking for the interpretation of his dreams and Joseph being the very one who could reveal to him the meaning of his dreams. I am raising up many 'Josephs' in this hour, and they

will not only be able to interpret dreams but will have the wisdom to implement them and bring order to situations, governments, and all manner of end-time events that will now take place.

"I have ordained a company of 'Daniels' who have discerned the end of the age and who will release My plans and implement them on this earth. They are full of wisdom and spiritual insights. They are not 'flaky' but have deep spiritual insight and discernment in what is happening on the face of this earth. Many will come to them for spiritual advice. They have My heart and My words in them, and many captives will be set free. Much that is in confusion and chaos will be brought back into divine order.

"I have prepared this company of wise leaders who will counsel those who have high positions in the nations of this world, and what will come forth will be no less than miraculous in many situations that are truly disastrous. Wisdom from on High will permeate their souls, and they will be filled with 'Light' from Heaven. I am now coming in ways that will 'startle' many, and they will wonder at the magnitude of this last Great Awakening!

"Get ready for these divine encounters, children, and know that dreams, visions, and miracles have already been released. Receive what I have for you, for I will anoint your eyes to see into the Spirit-realm in a measure you never have before. I will remove the blinders from your eyes and show you wonders that will take your breath away! These visitations will give you insight into what I am releasing in this hour, in your nation and in this world. This is a glorious season, not only for one nation but for many nations throughout this world, and I want to fill you and flow through you to this final generation that will experience My love and My power as no other generation ever has. Open your hearts and open your hands; open your eyes and ears, and see and hear and receive all that I have for you in this late hour—says your God!"

In this glorious *new era* there will be an increase in dreams and visions from the Lord. Where there has been an occasional dream or vision from the Lord, now there will be nightly revelations and dreams from the Spirit of God revealing secrets and giving direction to His people. The Spirit is calling all of God's children to come and to receive all that He has for them in this late hour. He is asking us to open our hearts and hands so that He can flood us with His glory. Jesus is giving His people greater discernment and revelation concerning the hour that we live in, and many are beginning to wake up. There will be angelic visitations and encounters with the Lord that will overwhelm God's children in this hour.

The Lord is raising up men and women who will release wisdom from on High and who will direct and give many leaders the wisdom and understanding that they need in order to govern and to lead their cities, states, and even nations in the direction that God desires them to go. They will be much like Joseph and Daniel of old, and they will astound the nations with the words they speak and the deeds that they perform in the name of Jesus. Doors of revelation and power are now opening, and all who come to Jesus will receive divine wisdom, not only for their own lives but for those around them, and this will keep many from falling into the trap of the enemy; God's people only need to ask. (See James 1:5.)

> After this I looked, and behold, a door standing open in heaven! And the first voice which I had heard, like the sound of a [war] trumpet speaking with me, said, "Come up here, and I will show you what must take place after these things." At once I was in [special communication with] the Spirit; and behold, a throne stood in heaven, with One seated on the throne.
> –Revelation 4:1–2

God is opening a *heavenly door* before His true children in this hour, a door into God's heavenly realm of power and of glory. Can you hear the Lord calling you to "Come up here" so that He can show you what is happening on the earth and what will happen in the days ahead? Jesus wants to commune with us, to show us what will take place in the future and to speak to us about the part we will play in the coming days. The One who is seated on the throne wants to commune with you and with me in this hour in a more profound way than we have ever known. We are "seated with Christ in heavenly places," and even now Jesus wants us to take our rightful place beside Him and begin to rule and reign with Him. (See Ephesians 2:6.)

> And it shall come to pass after this that I will pour out my Spirit upon all flesh; and your sons and your daughters shall prophesy, your old men shall dream dreams, your young men shall see visions: and even upon the slaves and upon the handmaids in those days will I pour out my spirit.
> –Joel 2:28–29 – JUB

These dreams and visions are not just for a "select few" but for **all** who will come to Him and surrender to His Lordship. The Spirit's desire is to pour out His blessing and His glory upon **all** flesh: both our sons and daughters and the young and the old. Many have longed for their wayward sons and daughters to experience the presence of God in powerful ways… to encounter Jesus through dreams and glorious visions. The Lord is no respecter of persons, but all who are "thirsty" and desire to receive more of Him will receive all that they hunger for in this hour. The question is: Are you hungry for more of God? More revelation? Do you desire to go deeper into the Spirit of God? If the answer is yes, then come, come to your Savior in your "quiet place," whether it be in your bedroom or your back yard; just come to Him, and He will satisfy the deepest yearnings in your soul.

> Where there is no vision [no revelation of God and His word], the people are unrestrained; but happy and blessed is he who keeps the law [of God].
> –Proverbs 29:18 – AMP

Those who do not have a vision from the Spirit and are just living day by day in their own thoughts and their own will, going their own way, are to be pitied. They live an empty, mundane life filled with the same routine day after day and believe that this is all that God has for them. I remember when I first came to Jesus; I was filled with great joy and anticipation concerning my future, for I knew that God had more for my life. But after a few years of walking and growing in the Spirit, I settled down to a life of *mediocracy* believing that going to church, reading my Bible, and doing a few good works would be enough to satisfy my soul, but it was not.

No one told me that the Lord had so much more for my life, and so my heart settled into a life of *complacency* and *spiritual boredom*. I loved the Lord, but my heart longed for so much more. Because of this lack of knowledge concerning my future, compromise and living by the "letter of the law" set in. I was not fulfilled neither was my heart filled with joy and expectancy in what God wanted to do in and through my life. Little did I realize that Jesus had so much more for my life. I was "unrestrained," living my life by my own standards and in my own will, but Jesus saw my empty heart. Through many fiery trials He awakened me to my calling and destiny in Him, and now I can say that my life is not "dull" but full of *expectancy*. The Spirit of God now leads and guides me. I live a life of obedience before Him, controlled by Him, and this is the place of true spiritual activity that is birthed in the Spirit. Now I live a life full of His presence as I listen to His voice daily and receive the fullness of His love.

> Surely the Lord GOD does nothing without revealing His secret plan [of the judgment to come] to His servants the prophets.
> –Amos 3:7

God has been revealing His "secret plans" to those who have "ears to hear" and to everyone who has set their hearts to seek Him above all the pleasures of this earth. A *door* is open before all who want to know what God is doing in this hour and who desire to have a greater and deeper discernment and revelation concerning the ways of God. The Spirit longs to reveal His secrets not only to His prophets but to all who are hungry and thirsty for the things of God. Everyone who opens their heart to Jesus in this *glorious new day* will receive greater revelations through dreams and visions and divine encounters. Get ready for new and glorious visitations that will take your breath away.

> In a dream, ***a vision of the night*** [one may hear God's voice], when deep sleep falls on men while slumbering upon the bed.
> –Job 33:15, emphasis added

Here we see that a dream can be called a "vision of the night," a time when we can hear the voice of God. God speaks to me a lot through nightly dreams, showing me what I'm struggling with, giving me discernment, revealing hidden sin, and showing me the things that are on the horizon, spiritually and on this earthly plane. During the night when we lay on our beds in stillness, God is then able to speak loud and clear to us through our dreams and to reveal to us all the things that we need to see and understand in our lives. This brings great peace to our soul and releases confusion from our hearts.

> Then the LORD answered me and said, "Write the vision and engrave it plainly on [clay] tablets so that the one who reads it will run."
> –Habakkuk 2:2

In my own life I have had hundreds of dreams from the Lord that were *not* "pizza dreams." Just because we don't understand them immediately when we wake up does not mean that they don't have deep spiritual meaning. There were times when I really believed that a dream didn't have any meaning until the Spirit of God gave me the interpretation, and then I would be amazed at what He was showing me. I have binders full of dreams that I have written out to look back on. When we show the Lord that we honor the dreams that He gives us, He will then increase them in our lives. The Scriptures below show us that dreams and visions were common-place from the beginning of time, so let's honor our God and thank Him for the revelations, dreams, and visions that He gives us.

And God spoke to Israel in visions of the night and said, "Jacob, Jacob!" And he said, "Here I am."
–Genesis 46:2

After these things the word of the Lord came to Abram in a vision, saying, "Do not be afraid, Abram, I am your shield; your reward [for obedience] shall be very great."
–Genesis 15:1

And they did not find His body. Then they came back, saying that they had even seen a vision of angels who said that He was alive!
–Luke 24:23

But God came to Abimelech in a dream during the night, and said, "Behold, you are a dead man because of the woman whom you have taken [as your wife], for she is another man's wife."
–Genesis 20:3

In the Scripture above we see that God will give a "warning" dream even to a "heathen" concerning a situation they may be ignorant of. Our God is kind and merciful to all and desires to communicate to His creation all the time, but most of the time even His children can't hear His voice because of all the activity they are involved in during the day. It takes a quiet heart in order to receive these "signals" and "messages" from Heaven. Let's thank the Lord for revealing so many things during the dark hours of the night. Dreams are truly a gift from the Lord.

It is necessary to boast, though nothing is gained by it; but I will go on to visions and revelations of the Lord. I know a man in Christ who fourteen years ago—whether in the body I do not know, or out of the body I do not know,

> [only] God knows—such a man was caught up to the third heaven. And I know that such a man—whether in the body or out of the body I do not know, [only] God knows—was caught up into Paradise and heard inexpressible words which man is not permitted to speak [words too sacred to tell].
>
> –2 Corinthians 12:1-4

The Apostle Paul had many dreams, visions, and encounters with His God. He was even caught up to the 3rd heaven. His experiences were so dramatic and inexpressible that he was given a "thorn" in his flesh so that he would not be lifted up in pride. We may not have the same experiences as Paul, but in our visitations and revelations we must also be given a "thorn" so that we will not think more highly of ourselves than we should. The Lord does not want us "puffed up," thinking that we are better than anyone else, so He will *allow* trials and testings to come our way in order to keep us at His feet in humility. God wants to give us so many more experiences in his Spirit, but we must be deeply "refined" in order to be *saved* from *ourselves.*

> But after he had considered this, an angel of the Lord appeared to him in a dream, saying, "Joseph, descendant of David, do not be afraid to take Mary as your wife, for the Child who has been conceived in her is of the Holy Spirit."
>
> –Matthew 1:20

There will be times when the Spirit of God will reveal to us in dreams or visions a confirmation of His will for our lives. Here we see that Joseph definitely needed a strong confirmation that he was to take Mary as his wife. Without this *night visitation* from the Lord, only God knows what decision Joseph would have made. We may not have as drastic a situation as Joseph, but there are times when we are in desperate situations and need to hear from the Lord. Many times God will reveal to us what to do and give us the wisdom that we need through a dream. Personally, I don't know where I would be if the

Lord didn't give me direction and discernment through the dreams He has given me. I encourage you to never take your dream life for granted but to pray and ask the Lord to sharpen your spiritual *night senses* as you dream. I believe God will begin to show you many things through them.

> But when Herod was dead, behold, the angel of the Lord appeared in dreams to Joseph in Egypt, saying, Arise and take the young child and his mother and go into the land of Israel, for they are dead who sought the death of the young child.
> –Matthew 2:19–20 – JUB

What would we do if God didn't give us direction? Many times, God will speak to us through the Word and also through the "still small voice" of the Spirit, but He will also speak clearly to us through our dreams and visions if we truly listen to them. God has not changed, for He is the same yesterday, today, and forever. He spoke to His people in dreams and visions in the past, and He hasn't changed His way of communicating with us in this hour. (See Hebrews 13:8.)

> As for these four young men, God gave them knowledge and skill in all kinds of literature and wisdom; Daniel also understood all kinds of visions and dreams.
> –Daniel 1:17 – AMP

The Spirit is raising up men and women who have an "excellent spirit" in this very generation. God is giving them divine discernment, skill, and wisdom that will confound many who believe that they are wise in the things of this world. Without God's understanding and wisdom this world would have perished long ago in the hands of ungodly men and women. The Lord has preserved this generation, and a company of Daniels are now coming to the forefront to move *mountains of darkness* out of the way through the power of the Spirit and the wisdom and the discernment that He has given them. These mighty men and women of God are able to interpret dreams and visions, and many will be astounded in what the Lord reveals through these servants of God.

> And they said to him, "We have [each] dreamed [distinct] dreams and there is no one to interpret them." So Joseph said to them, "Do not interpretations belong to God? Please tell me [your dreams]."
> –Genesis 40:8

God does not want only a certain few to be able to interpret dreams and visions, but all of His children who walk with Him in Truth can be given divine understanding in what God is revealing to them through their dream life. This *power to interpret dreams* comes from the Holy Spirit as we come to Him and spend time with Him in our place of solitude. We must *come to* the Lord and spend precious time with Him, listening to His voice and receiving from Heaven all that He desires to impart into our lives. Joseph and Daniel were men of prayer and submission to the will of the Lord, and this is why they had power and wisdom to interpret dreams and visions; they knew the heart of God in every situation that they faced. This does not come overnight but is developed as we read the Word, pray, and obey the Lord in every area of our lives.

> But there is a God in heaven who reveals secrets, and He has shown King Nebuchadnezzar what will take place in the latter days (end of days). This was your dream and the vision [that appeared] in your mind while on your bed.
> –Daniel 2:28

> And He said, "Hear now My words: If there is a prophet among you, I the Lord will make Myself known to him in a vision and I will speak to him in a dream."
> –Numbers 12:6

The Lord makes Himself known to all who are truly seeking Him in this hour. The prophet has a special calling in the 5-fold ministry, but all who are yielded and seeking Jesus with their whole heart will come to know the Lord in a deep and powerful way. The Lord will speak to every one who is thirsty for His love and presence, and He will speak to them powerfully through dreams and visions. As children of God, we must never take our dream life lightly, but always honor the presence of God, not only through the day but also through the night as we lay upon our beds. If you honor the Lord in this way, you will be astounded at what He will reveal to you in dreams and visions. The Spirit of God will reveal deep secrets and will amaze you with the "revelation knowledge" that He will impart to you during the night. I remember reading of how the Lord gave cures for illnesses and glorious inventions to men and women as they slept. Our God is amazing!

> Then a vision appeared to Paul in the night: a man from [the Roman province of] Macedonia was standing and pleading with him, saying, "Come over to Macedonia and help us!" And when he had seen the vision, we (including Luke) tried to go on into Macedonia at once, concluding that God had called us to preach the gospel to them.
> –Acts 16:9–10

I believe this is the day and the hour when thousands of God's people will be led by the Spirit through their dreams as God shows them where to go and what to do. So many are lost and need the message of salvation preached to them, but we must always be led by the Spirit of God, for He knows where the hungry souls are and what doors He wants opened before us. We must never be led by our own thinking or human understanding but rely completely on the Spirit to lead and to guide us in this hour. The hour is later than we think, and we cannot afford to waste the valuable time that God has given us. I pray we will always be led by the Spirit of God in all things and at all times.

This is my prayer for you: *"that your love may abound more and more in knowledge and depth of insight, so that you may be able to discern what is* best and may be pure and blameless for the day of Christ, filled with the fruit of righteousness that comes through Jesus Christ—to the glory and praise of God" (Philippians 1:9–11 – NIV).

Hear the voice of the Lord say:

"Hold tightly to My hand, for I am lifting you up into a heavenly realm of glory in this hour...a place of holiness, purity, and power...a place where you will 'know' Me in a greater depth of love and intimacy.

"You wonder: Where is this place? And how will I get there? This is the place where My glory dwells; this is the place that Isaiah saw, where My 'train' filled the temple, where all cry: 'Holy, holy, holy!' (See Isaiah 6:1–3.) This is the place that I am lifting you up to in this very hour, a High and Holy Place. My Spirit will lift you into this Place—this domain, where all is white, all is brilliant, and all is pure...a place where no evil can enter and only those who are truly Mine will know. This is the place that I am lifting you into. You will walk in this place; you will 'feast' with Me in this place. You will 'know' Me in this place, and you will never want to leave this place, for it will be to you the 'delight of your soul,' your place of love and joy and intimacy with Me. This is where you will abide in Me and are one with Me in every word, thought, and action. You think: Will this come to pass when I die physically and enter the 'gates of glory?' Yes, then you will know this in 'fullness,' but even now you can enter this place, live in this place, as I abide in you and you abide in Me.

"Many of My people have settled for so much less, and they feel empty and dry. They are unsatisfied with their present walk in My Spirit, and they believe that this is all that I have for them on this earth. What lies they have believed from the evil one! What a meager portion they have settled for! They experience no passion, no pleasure, and no power in My Spirit, but I say: 'Come up higher. Get up to higher ground, and take your place beside Me even now. Do not settle for less than what I have destined for you. Receive this larger portion of My Spirit and be filled with My joy and My ecstasy. I have so much more for you—so much more!'

"Delight in your God, and I will lift you up to this High and Holy Place, and you will know joy and ecstasy such as you have never known on this earthly plane. Come up higher; come up to Me and enjoy My pleasures now, My greater gifts and greater intimacy that I have prepared for you to enjoy even now on this earthly plane. Settle for nothing less. I will stir up, deep inside your soul, a greater hunger and thirst for Me, to 'know' Me, to love Me, and to receive all that I have for you.

"It will be so; it will be so: You will come up higher in this season— higher than you've ever known—says your God!"

The Bride Has Made Herself Ready

Who is this one? She arises out of her desert, clinging to her beloved. When I awakened you under the apple tree, as you were feasting upon me, I awakened your innermost being with the travail of birth as you longed for more of me. Fasten me upon your heart as a seal of fire forevermore. This living, consuming flame will seal you as my prisoner of love. My passion is stronger than the chains of death and the grave, all-consuming as the very flashes of fire from the burning heart of God. Place this fierce, unrelenting fire over your entire being. Rivers of pain and persecution will never extinguish this flame. Endless floods will be unable to quench this raging fire that burns within you. Everything will be consumed. It will stop at nothing as you yield everything to this furious fire until it won't even seem to you like a sacrifice anymore.

–Song of Solomon 8:5–7 – TPT

I love these Scriptures in the Passion Translation! The bride of Christ has come out of hiding, and she is leaning hard on Jesus, her Beloved. She is coming out of the wilderness, the dryness, the suffering, and she has learned that Jesus is her life, her love, her All in All. She has come out of the *flames of affliction* and has been purified and made ready to move forward with the Spirit into all that He has prepared for her to walk in. Her destiny is sure, and her identity in Christ is sealed. She has been conformed into the image of Jesus and is ready to bring in the harvest of souls that He is sending her forth to "reap." Her heart is burning with a passionate love for her Savior, and no one, no trial, no temptation will ever again quench this vehement love.

In this very hour the bride of Christ has been fully awakened to the love of Jesus. Her Beloved has satisfied her soul with the "wine" of His love. She has come to know His fierce, unrelenting fire over her whole body. Her innermost being has been awakened as she "travailed" before the Lord in brokenness, pouring out her heart to Him daily. And now this *living flame of love* from Jesus is burning deep in her heart. There is a raging, furious fire within her that no *flood* can quench; the love of Jesus has consumed her life.

She is a "prisoner" of His love, and she would not have it any other way! Jesus has consumed her in His love, and now all she wants is to please Him and to do His will above all. Her love for Jesus is so intense that nothing she goes through or anything He asks of her feels like a "sacrifice." Her delight is to do His will, for nothing brings her greater joy than to do His "bidding." The Spirit has purified her soul through all of her suffering and the fiery trials that she has endured, and she has come forth as pure gold. (See Job 23:10.) The bride of Christ knows that all the *delays,* all the *seeming denials,* and the *floods of affliction* she has gone through have not been in vain. She rejoices now in the passionate love of her Savior, and her heart is filled with joy and contentment in His glorious presence.

> For I am jealous for you with a godly jealousy; for I betrothed you to one husband, to present you as a pure virgin to Christ.
>
> –2 Corinthians 11:2 – NASB

> Husbands, love your wives, just as Christ also loved the church and gave Himself up for her, so that He might sanctify her, having cleansed her by the washing of water

> with the word, that He might present to Himself the church in all her glory, having no spot or wrinkle or any such thing; but that she would be holy and blameless.
>
> –Ephesians 5:25–27

Paul had a burning passion to present a bride "as a pure virgin" to Jesus, a bride without spot or wrinkle. Paul knew that sanctification and cleansing would come through the Word, the "Living Word," as it was applied to the lives of God's people. The Word of God not only washes us, but it is a "double-edged sword" that will pierce our hearts and expose what is unholy in us. (See Hebrews 4:12.) God's Word will "cut away" the darkness, the sin, and the iniquity from deep inside our hearts. We are sanctified by Truth, the truth of God's Holy Word, and Jesus is the "Living Word" that will wash out of our lives all that is not of Him. (See John 17:17.) This is the work of the Spirit in the hearts of God's people, for He alone can cleanse that deep place in our hearts and make all things new. The Spirit is the One who imparts the nature of Christ into our lives; this cannot be done in human strength or the wisdom of man.

> Now Abraham was old, well advanced in age; and the Lord had blessed Abraham in all things. So Abraham said to the oldest servant of his house, who ruled over all that he had, "Please, put your hand under my thigh, and I will make you swear by the Lord, the God of heaven and the God of the earth, that you will not take a wife for my son from the daughters of the Canaanites, among whom I dwell; but you shall go to my country and to my family, and take a wife for my son Isaac." And the servant said to him, "Perhaps the woman will not be willing to follow me to this land. Must I take your son back to the land from which you came?"
>
> –Genesis 24:1–5 – NKJV

The Father longs to give His Son a beautiful bride, and the Holy Spirit has found a *remnant* who passionately love Jesus and who have responded to this call. The Holy Spirit is the One who has drawn the bride of Christ into a deep love relationship with Jesus. For years the bride has been preparing her life in order to be *ready* for this *full union* with Jesus. She has one focus and one reason for living, and that is to be fully prepared for Him when He comes for her. She is willing to follow the Spirit as He leads and guides her into all that she must go through in order to be this *pure and spotless bride* for Jesus. She's been willing to go through the deep fires of purification and has not backed down before any "giant" that has tried to intimidate her. She's on her way to the "Promised Land," and no one will stop her from following the Lord all the way to her eternal home. Jesus is coming for a bride that looks like Him, walks like Him, and knows His heart. He will not marry anyone who loves this world and the things in it, but one who desires Him above all the pleasures of this earth.

> And it happened, before he had finished speaking, that behold, Rebekah, who was born to Bethuel, son of Milcah, the wife of Nahor, Abraham's brother, came out with her pitcher on her shoulder. Now the young woman was very beautiful to behold, a virgin; no man had known her. *And she went down to the well, filled her pitcher, and came up. And the servant ran to meet her and said, "Please let me drink a little water from your pitcher." So she said, "Drink, my lord." Then she quickly let her pitcher down to her hand, and gave him a drink. And when she had finished giving him a drink, she said, "I will draw water for your camels also, until they have finished drinking."* Then she quickly emptied her pitcher into the trough, ran back to the well to draw water, and drew for all his camels. And the man, wondering at her, remained silent so as to know whether the LORD had made his journey prosperous or not. So it was, when the camels had finished drinking, that the man took a golden nose ring weighing half a shekel, and two bracelets for her wrists weighing ten shekels of gold, and said, "Whose daughter are you?

Tell me, please, is there room in your father's house for us to lodge?"
—Genesis 24:15–23, emphasis added

Jesus arrived at the Samaritan village of Sychar, near the field that Jacob had given to his son Joseph. Wearied by his long journey, he sat on the edge of Jacob's well, and sent his disciples into the village to buy food, for it was already afternoon. **Soon a Samaritan woman came to draw water. Jesus said to her, "Give me a drink."**
—John 4:5–8 – TPT, emphasis added

The bride of Christ has been "laboring" hard for her King, working in His "vineyard," and doing His will. She has not been "idle" as others may have judged her. She has travailed in prayer and worked in *secret* accomplishing what the Lord has asked of her. She is filled with the *water* of the Word and has been quenching the "thirst" of those around her, those who would seek her out for advice and comfort. She has given freely to all who ask and has not held back from giving her all to Jesus. The Lord sees her as a beautiful "virgin," and though her past has been "tainted," Jesus has washed and cleansed her and filled her with His glory.

Jesus comes to His bride, and she satisfies His heart by giving Him "a drink," the love that she feels for Him as she worships before His throne. Many do not see or believe that Jesus desires their passionate worship filled with love-filled words and desire for Him. Jesus is "thirsty" for souls to come to Him and to pour out their love to Him, even as the Father desires His people to come and worship Him in Spirit and in Truth. Jesus' heart can only be fully satisfied as we spend time with Him in deep communion, opening our hearts fully to Him and receiving His deep and passionate love. Only then can we pour back to Him the "drink offering of love" that He so desires to receive from us.

Then I bathed you and washed off your blood, and I rubbed fragrant oils into your skin. I gave you expensive clothing of fine linen and silk, beautifully embroidered, and sandals made of fine goatskin leather. I gave you lovely jewelry, bracelets, beautiful necklaces, a ring for your nose, earrings for your ears, and a lovely crown for your head. And so you were adorned with gold and silver. Your clothes were made of fine linen and costly fabric and were beautifully embroidered. You ate the finest foods—choice flour, honey, and olive oil—and became more beautiful than ever. You looked like a queen, and so you were! Your fame soon spread throughout the world because of your beauty. I dressed you in My splendor and perfected your beauty, says the Sovereign Lord.

–Ezekiel 16:9–14 – NLT

The Lord has adorned His bride, His beloved, with "fine linen," His righteousness, and the costly "gifts" and "fruit" of the Spirit. (See 1 Corinthians 12:7–10; Galatians 5:22–23.) In Ezekiel's day they committed idolatry with the "gifts" and blessings that God gave them, and in the sight of God this was "prostitution." They were unfaithful to their God, and they dishonored the Lord their God, but Jesus has a bride who has remained faithful and true to Him. Jesus has adorned her with His beauty and is perfecting her in the *fire of His holiness.*

She has been "sealed" with the Holy Spirit as a "down payment" and will soon rise to meet her Bridegroom. (See Ephesians 1:13–16.) The Lord has washed her in His blood and has filled her with the "oil of the Spirit," and she is clean. Jesus' bride has eaten what is *good,* even the "Bread of Heaven," and has been conformed into the image of her Beloved. She is covered and filled with God's glory, and even now is walking as His queen, His bride, in regal splendor. The Lord is about to "unveil" His bride, and she will release God's miracle power into this dark and unbelieving world. This is the Lord's beautiful bride!

There are sixty queens and eighty concubines, and young women without number; but my dove, my perfect one,

> is unique: She is her mother's only daughter; she is the pure child of the one who gave birth to her. The young women saw her and called her blessed, the queens and the concubines also, and they praised her, saying, "Who is this who looks down like the dawn, as beautiful as the full moon, as pure as the sun, as awesome as an army with banners?"
> —Song of Solomon 6: 8–10 – NASB

The bride of Christ is unique, and in the eyes of her Beloved, she is perfect. She has been deeply purified and blessed beyond measure. Everyone will see that she has been "highly favored" and blessed by her King, much like Mary, and the presence of Jesus will be seen and manifested through her life powerfully. She will look like the "dawn," filled with the Light of the Spirit, and everywhere she goes darkness will be dispelled, and many will run to Jesus and cry out for His mercy and salvation.

> Then the servant brought out jewelry of silver, jewelry of gold, and clothing, and gave them to Rebekah. He also gave precious things to her brother and to her mother.
> —Genesis 24:53 – NKJV

> So they said, "We will call the young woman and ask her personally." Then they called Rebekah and said to her, "Will you go with this man?" And she said, "I will go."
> —Genesis 24:57–58

> Hear, O daughter, and consider, and incline your ear: forget your people and your father's house, and the king will desire your beauty. Since He is your lord, bow to him. The people of Tyre will seek your favor with gifts, the richest of the people. All glorious is the princess in her chamber, with robes interwoven with gold. In many-colored robes

she is led to the king, with her virgin companions following behind her. With joy and gladness they are led along as they enter the palace of the king.

–Psalm 45:10–15 – ESV

Not only was Rebekah adorned with riches, but her whole family was blessed because of her decision to go with Abraham's servant and to become Isaac's bride. In the same way when we are in covenant with God through Jesus' shed blood, God watches over our loved ones, and we know that we can trust Him to bring them safely home to Heaven. Our covenant with God cannot be broken as we walk in obedience to His will, and all that we have, including our loved ones, belong to Him. Our Father will care for them and will keep them from harm. I think of all the times that my heavenly Father delivered my loved ones from the enemy and even from physical harm, and it brings tears to my eyes. We can trust our God to keep His covenant promises, for He is faithful and will never fail us.

Rebekah said: *"Yes,"* and left everything behind in order to marry a man that she had never personally met, and in the same way the bride of Christ loves Jesus passionately even though she has not seen Him. (See 1 Peter 1:8.) Even now she loves her Bridegroom fervently, and she knows that this is only the beginning of their love relationship that will last throughout the eternal ages.

Jesus has greatly desired His bride to abandon all for Him and to come away with Him to the "High Place of Glory" that He has prepared for her. She will be brought to the King in "many-colored robes," and this always reminds me of Joseph's "coat of many colors." This is a *place of favor* for the Lord's bride, and because of her many trials and the suffering she has gone through, like Joseph, she is now all glorious within; her heart is pure, and her one passion is for Jesus. Jesus is truly her "first love."

Recently in prayer, the Lord began to speak to me about the love relationship between a soon-to-be bride and her future husband. Jesus showed me that when a couple is preparing for their wedding day, they are completely focused on preparing for that glorious time when their union will be complete. They are making plans for the wedding ceremony, and there is much time spent making calls and arrangements for the glorious wedding day that they will enjoy. They are also spending much time together, and their hearts are beating as one as the *day of their bliss* nears. Everything else in the world is fading away as their passion and their love for each other grows daily, and they can hardly contain their joy when their wedding day finally arrives. As they anticipate their wedding day, so great is their love for one another and their longing to be fully united that "a day seems as a thousand years." (See 2 Peter 3:8.)

Many of God's people do not realize that Jesus is passionately in love with them and that He longs for His people to come close to Him so that He can reveal the intensity of His love toward them. They are happy *just to make it* to Heaven someday and do not realize that Jesus is calling and preparing a bride for the "Marriage Supper of the Lamb." These are days of intense preparation, and the Lord is drawing His people through fiery trials and suffering in order to prepare them for this glorious "feast." Even now the Spirit is drawing God's children to see who is willing to say: *"Yes"* to this glorious end-time call to be the "bride of Christ."

The true "bride of Christ" feels an even greater and more intense love for Jesus than an engaged couple feels, and she longs for the day of His appearing when He will take her to the "place that He has prepared for her." (See John 14:2–3.) She has walked with her Beloved on this earthly plane and can hardly contain the joy she is feeling, for she knows that soon she will be going home with her Beloved King to enjoy His love in a way that will overwhelm her. She has longed for years to know the fullness of who He is and to know the fullness of His embrace, and now she knows that this *day of bliss* is drawing near. She has not longed or looked for other "loves," but her heart has been focused on Him alone, and she has prepared her heart and life for the fullness of this glorious union with her Bridegroom.

Many in the Body of Christ are not prepared for the Lord's "appearing" neither do they passionately long for His embrace. Jesus is *not* their "first love," for the things of this world have distracted them and have kept them from loving Jesus in the way that He desires them to. But I believe that all of this is changing, for many have already answered His passionate cry to come to Him in this dark hour. Jesus has been revealing His heart of love to many, many hearts who are longing for fulfillment and satisfaction in this very generation. The *fires of tribulation* have opened many closed hearts to Jesus' love, and I believe we will see millions more come to the Lord as these "fires" intensify on the earth.

> Now Isaac pleaded with the LORD for his wife, because she was barren; and the LORD granted his plea, and Rebekah his wife conceived…So when her days were fulfilled for her to give birth, indeed there were twins in her womb.
> –Genesis 25:21, 24 – NKJV

The Lord's "desolate ones" will now break forth and sing for joy "for the [spiritual] sons of the desolate one will be more numerous than the sons of the married woman" (Isaiah 54:1b – AMP). The bride of Christ will now realize that the Lord has kept His *best* for her, even giving her more spiritual sons and daughters than she could ever dream He would. She has felt desolate and barren, spiritually, but now she will be the joyful "mother" of many spiritual children. Her sadness and depression will be turned into greatest joy as she realizes that Jesus has given her a double-portion, much like what was given to Job after he went through numerous trials that tested his faith. Her days have been "fulfilled," and now she will birth the fullness of her calling and destiny in Christ.

> "Let's rejoice and be glad and give the glory to Him, because the marriage of the Lamb has come, and His bride has prepared herself." It was given to her to clothe herself in fine linen, bright and clean; for the fine linen is the righteous acts of the saints. Then he said to me, "Write: 'Blessed are those who are invited to the wedding feast of the Lamb.'" And he said to me, "These are the true words of God."
> –Revelation 19:7–9 – NASB

The "Marriage Supper of the Lamb" is coming sooner than most are expecting, and those who have been spending time with Jesus have prepared their hearts and their lives for this great wedding feast. Their wedding garments have no "spots or wrinkles" on them, for they have been cleansed from the defilement of this world. They are, even now, dressed in "fine linen" because they walk in His "righteous acts" in obedience to His will and are "following the Lamb" wherever He goes. They have fully prepared their lives and have been released from the shame and the grief of their past. They know His joy; they know His love, and their hearts, even now, are united with their King. They walk in His ways and know His thoughts. They are *one* in everything they say and do, and they know that they are blessed!

> My beloved spoke, and said to me: "Rise up, my love, my fair one, and come away. For lo, the winter is past, the rain is over and gone. The flowers appear on the earth; the time of singing has come, and the voice of the turtledove is heard in our land. The fig tree puts forth her green figs, and the vines with the tender grapes give a good smell. Rise up, my love, my fair one, and come away!"
> –Song of Solomon 2:10–13 – NKJV

Can you hear the love call of Jesus in this hour beckoning you to rise up out of your pain and your grief and come away with Him? Your "winter of suffering" is over, and He is calling you to come up higher and to "feast" with Him as He pours out torrential *rivers of love* into your entire being. Jesus is calling you to come and to "dine" with Him, for He has a "love feast" that He wants you to enjoy so that you can have the assurance that you are fully prepared to meet with Him face-to-face.

The *flood of trials* you have been in have subsided, and you will now experience the warmth of His love and His restoration in every area of your life. As you come to Jesus and open your heart fully to Him, pouring out everything that has hurt you and kept you from knowing His destiny and calling for your life, you will be filled with a new song of joy as you enter into your *new day!* Hear His voice this day and rise up; let go of your life fully. Come away with Jesus and know the fullness of His love for you!

Listen to what the Bridegroom is saying:

> *"Your winter is over, and your spring has arrived. (See Song of Solomon 2:11–12.) Rise up, My beloved, My fair one, My bride, and come away with Me. Let Me hear the sound of your voice; let Me see your face, for it is beautiful My 'dove,' My fair one. (See Song of Solomon 2:10, 14.)*
>
> *"There is **only one** that I have set My gaze upon. My bride, come near to Me, for I am calling you to come closer to Me, closer than you ever have before. (See Song of Solomon 6:8–9.) My beloved bride, can you hear My voice calling out to you to rise up and know that the 'drought,' the 'coldness,' and your years of emptiness are over? This is a **new day** for you, a day of joy and of celebration, a day of joyful singing, and a day of gathering in the full harvest of souls that belong to My Kingdom. You have sown many tears; now receive your reward: a harvest of righteousness in your life and a time of great satisfaction as millions of souls enter into My Kingdom. Your tears of sorrow have dried up, and now you will weep only tears of joy and laughter, for what has been 'planted,' My 'seeds' of Truth and love for many years, will now spring forth in faith and love and joy.*
>
> *"You will be sent to the nations, and you will see countless souls run into My Kingdom. This is harvest time, My beloved; this is the time of singing and endless joy, and nothing, no one will ever rob you of your joy and praise in My goodness ever again.*
>
> *"You have worked hard through your long, hard 'spiritual winter,' but you have now entered into a **new day** of glorious rejoicing as you bring in the 'sheaves' and receive untold blessings that you will now enjoy. (See Psalm 126:6.) Your 'labor' has not been in vain but have been for Me, for souls, and for 'birthing' the **new things** that will now come forth from your life. Nothing has been in vain; not one tear, not one cry has been overlooked by Me, My beloved, for I have prepared you for this very time and season, for this 'Great Awakening' that is now upon your nation and this world.*

*"You have believed My promises, and now you will see just how blessed you are. You have not only **believed** for the fulfillment of My promises, but now you will receive all that I have promised you through your many years of sorrow. The cost has been great, but My reward is so much greater...so much greater, My beloved one. Begin to walk now in the fullness of this new Life that is coming forth from you and receive the glory, power, love, and joy that will now break forth within your soul and body.*

"This is the season of fulfillment for those who have believed and have stood on My promises when their whole world was 'shaken' and darkness tried to overtake them. This is the generation of My 'awakened' ones who will now go forth and awaken countless millions of souls in this very generation.

"Your tears have been My 'seeds' planted in the 'soil' of many hearts, and these chosen, end-time souls will now come forth as these 'seeds' of truth and life break open in their hearts and they at last see My Light and My Glory and run to Me, their Savior and their God."

The Wedding Feast of Cana – The Third Day

*"You will come now to a refreshing oasis...a place of refreshing and renewal. Come to Me and drink these refreshing waters. They are for you, and you will feel My strength and My power fill you to overflowing. This is a **new day,** and I have **new things** for you, **new assignments,** a **new mantle,** and **a new place of authority and power** that I want you to step into. You will see Me face-to-face and will know that I have not forgotten you, and you will be thrilled down into the 'core' of your being. You will feel My presence fill you in a manner you have never known in the past.*

*"Nothing in this **new era** will move you, for you will come into a fullness of power that will strengthen you and will fill you to overflowing. What you have seen and known in your past is all fading away, and My glory will now permeate, not only your entire being but will be manifested in all that surrounds you: all of your*

circumstances and everything that touches your life. I am taking full control of all that touches your life and all that concerns you, and truly, you will see that I am seated on the 'throne' of your heart.

"You will no longer feel helpless or alone; your wilderness days are over, and you have stepped into a <u>new day,</u> for behold, I say even now: 'I make all things new' in your life. No more days of darkness and depression, no matter how dark it is all around you. The enemy has no part in you, and you will soar with Me in the heavenlies and know that you are 'seated with Me in heavenly places.'

"What has been **lost** in your life will now be **found** in a greater measure than before, even a 100-fold harvest of blessing. All is being restored back to you, and you will find Me in every moment of your day and night. Trust Me as I finish quickly these last 'strokes' of My brush upon your life. These are 'strokes' of glory and power, not doom and gloom.

"There will no longer be days and nights of sorrow and fatigue, for your days of weakness are over! Now you will experience My strength and what I will do through your life in this very generation. In the past you struggled in your weakness to do even the simplest of things, for the enemy tried to weigh you down and even stop you from moving into the fullness that I planned for your life. Now you will see and experience what it means to have 'satan under your feet.' (See Romans 16:20.) You know who you are, for your identity in Me is firmly established in your soul. You are bold and courageous and no longer fear facing your most violent enemy. You have crossed over into My 'Promised Land,' and now you are experiencing the 'blessed' life because you have **believed the promises** that I have spoken to you in the past.

"Step forward now and take every last promise that I have spoken to you. It is a **new day;** these are glory days, and you will joy in the fullness of My love and My presence in your life. It has arrived: days of power and of glory beyond words to express. Take all that I have for you now. Be vigilant; be violent, and 'take the Kingdom by force' (see Matthew 11:12), for you are My true ambassador in this **new season of glory**—says your God!"

> On the ***third day*** there was a wedding in Cana of Galilee, and the ***mother of Jesus*** was there. Now both Jesus and His disciples were invited to the wedding. And when they ran out of wine, the mother of Jesus said to Him, "They have no wine." Jesus said to her, "Woman, what does your concern have to do with Me? My hour has not yet come." His mother said to the servants, "Whatever He says to you, do it." Now there were set there six waterpots of stone, according to the manner of purification of the Jews, containing twenty or thirty gallons apiece. Jesus said to them, "Fill the waterpots with water." And they filled them up to the brim. And He said to them, "Draw some out now, and take it to the master of the feast." And they took it. When the master of the feast had tasted the water that was made wine, and did not know where it came from (but the servants who had drawn the water knew), the master of the feast called the bridegroom. And he said to him, "Every man at the beginning sets out the good wine, and when the guests have well drunk, then the inferior. You have kept the good wine until now!"
>
> –John 2:1–10, emphasis added

On September 29, 2019 at sundown (Rosh Hashanah), we moved into the Jewish year 5780. The Lord showed me that beginning with the Jewish year 5780 and our year of 2020, we entered into a *decade of glory,* a 10-year span of unprecedented miracles and an outpouring of glory that this world has never seen that will surpass all past revivals, but that it would also be a time of warfare, darkness, and judgment. I have expounded on this topic in my book: "The God of War" if you would like to know more about this glorious decade that we have entered into.

We also have entered into the 3rd 1,000-year millennium from the time that Jesus walked on the earth. With the Lord "one day is as a thousand years." (See 2 Peter 3:8.) This is the time when God will release the "3rd Great Awakening" that so many of God's people have longed for, and I believe it will start with the Church, God's very own children. Jesus showed me that many who go to church in this hour have never had a *true* encounter with Him. Thousands have not truly given their hearts and lives to Jesus but have found the Church to be a place of entertainment and comfort, not a place of true and deep repentance and a true surrender to the will of the Father. But all of this is about to change as they encounter the true miracle-working power of the Spirit and as they encounter the living Christ. Many in this generation have no true "wine," but now, in this 3rd day *awakening*, multitudes will at last see and receive true salvation and the love, the "wine," of Jesus into their hearts and lives.

It was on the *3rd day* that there was a wedding feast in Cana, and many are crying out to Jesus in this hour because they have no more "wine." They feel that their love has "dried up" because of their wilderness experience and the many trials they have gone through in these past years. They have been faithful to the Lord and have poured out to others consistently, and now they need a time of refreshing and renewal in this *new day* that they have entered into. Their lives, as represented by the "waterpots" in these Scriptures, are empty, and they are crying out for an outpouring of the Spirit to fill and to renew their lives. Many of God's children feel *weary* and *empty* and do not realize that it is the Lord that has emptied their lives of the things of this world in order to fill them full of His glory, the "Water of His Spirit" in this very hour!

Mary is the one who came to Jesus and told Him that they had "no more wine," but Jesus already knew that. In the same way the bride of Christ is crying out to the Lord for the Church because of its desolate and powerless condition. The bride is crying out for a new and fresh outpouring of the Spirit upon the Church and for a great awakening and revelation of the love and reality of the living Christ. The "bride of Christ" knows that we have entered into the *third day*, the time when we will see the greatest outpouring of the Spirit that this world has ever seen. Even though the Lord told his mother that His time had not yet come, Mary still had faith to believe that Jesus would perform this glorious miracle. Jesus responded to her strong faith and released this powerful miracle. Jesus has kept the best wine, the most glorious outpouring of His love, for this very generation. We are a privileged people of God to have been chosen to live in this very *decade of glory*, this *3rd Great Awakening*.

I love Mary's strong faith, for after she spoke to her Son about them not having any more wine, she then immediately told the servants that "whatever He says to you, do it." She already knew that Jesus would perform this miracle, and so does the "bride of Christ" have faith that Jesus will perform glorious miracles in this *decade of glory*. She knows that her Beloved hears her voice and that she is speaking His will when she prays concerning this last great outpouring. Her heart is one with Jesus, and she feels His longing and passion for the Church and for this very generation. She is bold in her faith, even as Mary was when she spoke to her Son concerning the empty "water-pots." What an example of faith Mary was and is to us in this very hour.

Even as Mary told the servants to "do whatever He says," in the same way we are to walk in full obedience and do whatever Jesus tells us to do. The Lord will reveal many things to us in this hour and may ask us to do some unusual and extraordinary things for Him. We must obey Him, no matter what other people say or think concerning what He asks of us. Obeying the will of God must be top priority in our lives and everything else *secondary* if we are to walk in His miracle power and glory. Jesus will give us all that we need to accomplish His will, no matter how big or how small the *mission* is that He sends us on. The Lord will supply our every need, and we will go forth in full faith with no fear or trepidation. We will be bold and strong and do all that He requires of us, for truly this season will be short, and there is much to accomplish in bringing in this final harvest of souls.

> Come and let us return [in repentance] to the LORD, for He has torn us, but He will heal us; He has wounded us, but He will bandage us. After two days He will revive us; on the **third day** He will raise us up that we may live before Him. So let us know and become personally acquainted with Him; let us press on to know and understand fully

the [greatness of the] Lord [to honor, heed, and deeply cherish Him]. His appearing is prepared and is as certain as the dawn, and He will come to us [in salvation] like the [heavy] rain, like the spring rain watering the earth.
–Hosea 6:1–3 – AMP, emphasis added

Again, we hear the word: "Come" and a plea to return to the Lord. Many of God's children have been "torn," but this is the hour to be made *whole* in every area of our lives. Jesus has put us through many fiery trials, and we have come forth purified and whole. If you read these Scriptures carefully, you will see that the Lord is the One who has torn us; He is the One who has wounded us, but He is also the One who will heal us. Nothing will keep us from His healing power in this hour, and all who come to Jesus will know that nothing is too hard for Him.

We have entered the 3rd day, and it is time to be revived and raised up into the new place that the Lord has for us. We shall now live in His "sight," His presence, in a new and glorious way, for the Lord will manifest His glory to us in astounding ways, in ways that will take our breath away. It is time to press into the Lord's heart even more deeply than we ever have… to know and to understand fully the greatness of our God. "His appearing is prepared and as certain as the dawn," and I believe that NOW is the time when we will experience the "heavy flood" of His presence. This last great outpouring is going to overwhelm us bringing both His judgments and His glory. This will be the *best of times* for God's true children, but the *worst of times* for the wicked and for those who refuse to repent.

But God raised Him on the **third day** and made Him to appear.
–Acts 10:40 – ESV, emphasis added

Jesus was raised up on the 3rd day, and in the same way, those who have been in a grave of "dead dreams" and great loss will now be raised up into the *new things* that God has for their lives. Those who have been hidden in a "wilderness of preparation" will now come forth; it is time for their "appearing." Jesus is going to lift up His bride and reveal His glory and works through her life. This is the day when He will appear in and through His beloved. Everyone will see and know that it is "Christ in her" that performs the miracles and wonders that come forth from her life. (See Colossians 1:27.)

> On the ***third day*** Esther put on her royal robes and stood in the inner court of the king's palace, in front of the king's quarters, while the king was sitting on his royal throne inside the throne room opposite the entrance to the palace.
>
> –Esther 5:1, emphasis added

In this glorious 3rd day the bride of Christ will put on her "royal robes" and stand in the "inner court," "behind the veil," and she will know that she is "seated in heavenly places with Christ." (See Ephesians 2:6.) She will walk in regal splendor as Jesus leads and guides her day by day to the places where He wants His glory revealed. Out of her "belly will flow rivers of living water," and millions will be freed from their lifelong captivity. (See John 7:38). The breath of God will come forth as she speaks the *whole counsel* of God, and many will weep great tears of repentance as the Spirit "uncovers" them and they see that selfishness and compromise control their lives. They will see that many idols have taken the place of their love relationship with Jesus and that they have left their "first love." Like Queen Esther, God will flow through them to save a generation that has gone astray and a Church that "evil Haman" (the adversary) is intent on destroying.

The Heart of Jesus says:

> *"Look only to Me to fulfill and to satisfy every love-need in your life. You have drawn close to Me; now come closer, and you will feel My 'Breath of Life' upon you. I will breathe on you, and you will 'resurrect' into the full life, love, and power that I have ordained for you to walk in. My grace is sufficient for you, and My love is all-powerful. My power is able to break through every barrier and every hindrance that has tried to block your entrance into this new place of glory that I have prepared for you. My*

grace has been sufficient for you in the past, and now you will experience that final breakthrough that you have so longed for. I am coming in great power to release you in a way that you are not expecting, in a way you are not even looking for.

"Am I not your All-Powerful God? Have I not cared for you and loved you in ways that you never expected? Will I not continue to come to you in new and exciting ways? You are My love-child...the one I have chosen to fill with My love, glory, and power. You will not be left desolate but will now come forth out of your 'cocoon' in a greater love and power than you could ever dream or imagine. The glory and power in your 'spiritual wings' will take you to many new places, near and far. You will soar with Me to new heights of glory, and your feet will land in the places that I will send you to. Many will say: 'She has winged feet,' for you will move swiftly with the Lord your God and accomplish much in a very short time.

"Children, you have come to a place where all of My works, in and through your life, will be accelerated exponentially, and no man...no devil will stop this work, for it will be accomplished quickly and precisely according to My perfect will and pattern—the pattern that I have ordained for your life, the lives of My people, and for this entire earth. Look now for this acceleration in your life, for you are about to take off in a way that will amaze and even startle you!

"Never have I loved you more. Never has My heart been more thrilled with what I am bringing you into. My passion and My glory in you are about to ***explode*** *in a way that will overwhelm you and will bring many more souls into My Kingdom. This* ***glory explosion*** *inside of you will draw multitudes into My Kingdom, and nothing in this world will hold you back or hinder your love-walk with Me ever again.*

"Love is the key. Love is the 'element' that I will measure your life with. Love believes all things and hopes all things. (See 1 Corinthians 13:7.) Love is what will draw souls to Me like a strong 'magnet,' a force of power that no one and nothing on this earth can compare. You will see, you will feel this strong love-magnet in your life now, and many, many souls will be drawn to My irresistible love in this hour."

> "Turn back, and say to Hezekiah the leader of my people, thus says the LORD, the God of David your father: I have heard your prayer; I have seen your tears. Behold, I will heal you. On the ***third day*** you shall go up to the house of the LORD.
>
> –2 Kings 20:5, emphasis added

In this great *turnaround era* God is going to "turn back" to His people and bring a flood of His *healing power* to the multitudes. The Lord has heard our cries for this generation. He has seen our tears and our travail, and in this 3rd day we will see a release of His healing power in a measure that no other generation has seen. Many will return to the "house of the Lord" and know that God is moving in power to set them free. A renewed hunger and thirst will be released inside the hearts of millions, and we will, I believe, see churches opened 24/7 in the days ahead because of continual prayer and passionate worship.

> I know your deeds. See, I have set before you an open door which no one is able to shut, for you have a little power, and have kept My word, and have not renounced or denied My name.
>
> –Revelation 3:8 – AMP

God is opening "doors" for us in this hour, both spiritually and physically. Jesus has opened up to us the *door of Heaven,* and in this 3rd day we will walk under an open Heaven continually. Dark, demonic "veils" and "strongholds" that have *covered* and *bound* cities, states, and nations will now be removed as God's glory is released and millions of souls are gloriously set free from their sin and iniquities. I believe this will happen *suddenly,* even as it did in the days of Hezekiah. (See 2 Chronicles 29:36.) The Spirit is going to open doors that have been shut to us for many years, and we will have ministry opportunities that we never dreamed we would have. Jesus told me that we are going to *run* with Him because He is going to complete a mighty work in a very short time. Jesus completed His mission in 3 years, and I believe that the Lord is going to complete His work through us in a very short span of time.

> But you [still] have a few people in Sardis who have not soiled their clothes [that is, contaminated their character and personal integrity with sin]; and they will walk with Me [dressed] in white, because they are worthy (righteous). He who overcomes [the world through believing that Jesus is the Son of God] will accordingly be dressed in white clothing; and I will never blot out his name from the Book of Life, and I will confess and openly acknowledge his name before My Father and before His angels [saying that he is one of Mine].
> –Revelation 3:4–5

God has a remnant that has been "washed" fully in the blood of the Lamb, and she is ready to move with Him in this hour. His bride may not "feel" fully prepared, but God has her right where He wants her. She is fully dependent on Him and follows Him wherever He leads her. The hearts of His "chosen" have been purified, and their characters have been refined. They walk with Jesus in "white," even now, and have overcome this world. Jesus is now her very life, her breath, and all of Heaven rejoices over His bride as she walks in the Spirit's overcoming power. She is filled with the love of Jesus and has found His presence all-satisfying. Nothing in this world can pull her away from her Beloved Jesus, for she is already enjoying the "new wine" of Jesus' love, and her "water-pot," her heart and life, is filled to overflowing with the presence of the One she loves more than life. Her joy is to do whatever He asks of her, for she delights to do His will above all the pleasures of this earth. This is the 3rd day, and this is the beautiful and obedient "bride of Christ!"

> Now all glory to God, who is able to keep you from falling away and will bring you with great joy into His glorious presence without a single fault. All glory to Him who alone is God, our Savior through Jesus Christ our Lord. All glory,

majesty, power, and authority are His before all time, and in the present, and beyond all time! Amen.

–Jude 1:24–25 –NLT

The Spirit says:

"All is in My hands and My hands alone, and I have found a remnant who will walk with Me and will decree into the earth My whole will and desire for this nation and every nation on this earth. These warriors will not back down from their stance of faith but are determined to see My full will come forth into this generation. At last I have seen and known a people who are truly Mine—who stand together as one in faith and trust in Me and My Word. I have waited long for this final remnant of Believer's to come forth out of 'hiding' and to walk with Me in full obedience to My will.

"You will see them now, for these are My 'firebrands.' These are the ones who will shake the whole earth with My glory and My power. They do not care what man says about them neither will they be moved, no matter what comes against them, for they have already 'died,' and nothing, no one can touch them or move them from their stance of faith in Me. I have grown strong in them through years and years of intense warfare, criticism, fear, and confusion, but they have stood firm and would not back down. They continued to push back the darkness in their hearts and their minds and have stood on My Truth until they were no longer shaken by the lies and pressures of the evil one.

"They have 'worked out' their faith in fear and in trembling and have loved Me more than their own lives. These are the ones I have chosen. This is My chosen bride that will stand with Me throughout the eternal ages. They will rule and reign with Me and will know that I have loved them. I will shower them with untold blessing, and many will wonder at the magnitude of power and glory they will walk in. Even now they are beginning to walk in 'regal' splendor.

"These are My Esther's, My Paul's, My Peter's...My blessed group of sold-out lovers who will now begin to walk in the High Glory and Power that I have ordained for them to walk in. This is My bride, My beloved, My uncompromised lover who has abandoned all for My sake and for the sake of My Kingdom.

"This world will stand in awe and in wonder as they see My bride move and shake this world, awaken those in the Church who have fallen asleep, spiritually, and release bound souls on the earth who have not known My love and My mercy. Oh, yes, this 'bridal company' is even now walking with Me in 'white.' They have paid the price and laid down their lives for Me completely and are even now enjoying My resurrected Life inside of their souls. They know Me, truly know Me and love Me above all the things in this world. They are My champions who will now 'take by force' the Kingdom and begin to rule and reign with Me on this earth in this very hour."

My prayer for you is: "that you may walk worthy of the Lord, fully pleasing Him, being fruitful in every good work and increasing in the knowledge of God; strengthened with all might, according to His glorious power, for all patience and longsuffering with joy" (Colossians 1:10–11 – NKJV).

CONCLUSION

As we come to the end of this book, I want to encourage those who may still be struggling to stand on the promises that God has made to you. The Spirit of God is still working in your heart and your life, and in His perfect, Kairos time, you **will** experience your breakthrough **if** you don't faint. Keep trusting and keep believing, for your reward is right before you!

> And let us not be weary in well-doing: for in due season we shall reap, if we faint not.
>
> –Galatians 6:9 – ASV

God reminded me as I was seeking Him concerning the conclusion of this book about Job and all of the suffering and confusion he went through. Some of you may be in that place, not understanding why you are going through such difficult times. I, too, went through that dark valley, and I promise you: As you keep your focus on Jesus and continue to trust and praise Him in the midst of the darkness, you WILL come through to the other side, your new day.

Job suffered horrendous losses, and God "allowed" the adversary to try and to test him. (See Job 1:6–12.) Job was a righteous man, but the Lord wanted to give Job a greater revelation of His glory and His power; God wanted to bring him up to higher ground…to a place of absolute trust in Him. After his fiery trials Job came forth as pure gold, and God rewarded him with a double-portion blessing at the end of his "ordeal." This is what Jesus is working out in all who are trusting Him and standing in faith in this hour.

> But He knows where I am going. And when He tests me, I will come out as pure as gold.
>
> –Job 23:10 – NLT

I believe the Book of Job was written for every soul who questions God's ways in the midst of their dark trials. After all of Job's questionings, self-pity, grief, loss, pain, and physical suffering, God answered him out of the whirlwind. (See Job 38:1.) God didn't come to Job and answer all of his questions, all of his whys, but God revealed to him His omnipotence and sovereignty, His full control over all that had happened in his life.

The Lord was after Job's heart and wanted him to trust Him fully and completely apart from his own understanding and reasoning. We do not come to this place without a "fight of faith" and some "bumps" and "bruises," but in God's grace we, too, can come to a place of absolute trust in our sovereign God and know, without a shadow of a doubt, that He loves us perfectly and will work out His will in our lives for our ultimate good and for His glory even though for a season we will go through various trials.

> This command I entrust to you, Timothy, my son, in accordance with the prophecies previously made concerning you, that by them you fight the good fight.
> –1 Timothy 1:18 – NASB

The Lord wants to remind you and me not to "kick against the "goads." (See Acts 26:14.) *"The phrase 'kicking against the goads' was a common expression in Bible times, referring to the practice of farmers goading their oxen in the fields. A goad is defined as a spiked stick used for driving cattle or oxen. According to Chuck Swindoll, there were occasions when an ox would kick at the goad. When this happened, the goad would stab into the flesh of its leg and cause greater pain."*[xxvi]

There will be times in our lives when God will take us though some deep waters and speak words to us that may bring pain and confusion, but we must *continue* to stand on His promises and not pull back in unbelief. If we "kick against the goads" we will only prolong the "process" that the Lord wants to take us through. If we embrace our cross and trust Jesus fully, we will avoid unnecessary pain and come through our "wilderness" more quickly.

Jesus is speaking to us in this hour to stand firm on every promise and every word that He has spoken to us and to wage the "good warfare."

We must **not** *back down* but *take back* from the enemy everything that he has robbed us of in the past. This is a *new day,* saints of God, and the Spirit's desire is to overwhelm you with His presence and His glory. Get ready to receive all that Jesus has promised you, and so much more!

> Let us hold fast the confession of our hope without wavering, for He who promised is faithful.
> –Hebrews 10:23 – NKJV

> For all the promises of God in Him are Yes, and in Him Amen, to the glory of God through us.
> –2 Corinthians 1:20

JESUS – THE YES AND AMEN!
By Theresa Reyna

You're the *Yes* and the *Amen,* Lord – Your promises are true,
We stand upon your Word – as You make all things new!
We stand now in faith – in the high, stormy gale,
For we know as we trust You – Your Word cannot fail.
You've promised us glory – if we stand firm and strong
All through the night – no matter how long!
Lord, You won't fail us – we're willing to wait,
Your Word is the Truth – we're not given to fate!
We must put down the doubts – our fears and our pain,
We'll receive these great promises – for our faiths' not in vain.
In Your love we will see – our desires come to pass,
And we'll shout *"Hallelujah"* – for we'll see You at last!
For You are our Lord – our hearts deepest desire,
<u>You</u> are the One – who lifts us out of the mire!
You're the Alpha and the Omega – the First and the Last,
All is now glorious – gone is our past!
Come, now, Lord Jesus – reveal Your glory to us,

For You alone we have waited – and in You is our trust.
Your Word has made us strong – in You we delight,
In the midst of these battles – You've won every fight!
Our minds are renewed – in Your Holy Word,
We say *"Yes"* and *"Amen"* – as we pick up our sword!
We go forth now in power – and cut the enemy down,
No more in great sorrow – no more with a frown!
Great joy fills our heart – in this very hour,
We go forth in Your Spirit – and Your overcoming power!
We're no longer the <u>tail</u> – but in You we're the <u>head</u>,
We'll now see the enemy – at our feet fall as dead!
You're our conquering Hero – we stand tall in You,
We're Your remnant, dear Lord – Your chosen few!
You've anointed and sealed us – for Your heavenly plans,
To follow Your Spirit – <u>not</u> the ways of man!
We're established in You – to do Your good will,
Lift us up to the top – of Your Holy Hill!
We vow Lord to walk – in <u>all</u> Your commands,
As You send us forth now – into dark, heathen lands!
Preaching and teaching – as onward we press,
Saying "<u>Amen</u>" to Your Word – and to You always "<u>YES!</u>"

Bibliography

i. Bricker, Vivian. "Do We Know How Old Mary Was When She Had Jesus?" *Christianity.com*, Christianity.com, https://www.christianity.com/wiki/holidays/do-we-know-how-old-mary-was-when-she-had-Jesus.html. Accessed 24 February 2022.

ii. Irwin, Sarah. "Joachim and Anne, Parents of the Blessed Virgin Mary." *GrowChristians.org*, Grow Christians, https://www.growchristians.org/2019/07/26/joachim-and-anne-parents-of-the-blessed-virgin-mary/. Accessed 24 February 2022.

iii. "1982. Episkiazó." *BibleHub.com*, Bible Hub, https://biblehub.com/greek/1982.htm. Accessed 24 February 2022.

iv. "Fellowship." BibleStudyTools.com, Bible Study Tools, https://www.biblestudytools.com/dictionaries/bakers-evangelical-dictionary/fellowship.html. Accessed 13 March 2022.

v. Singh, S. Sundar. "I Have Decided to Follow Jesus." *Library.TimelessTruths.org*, Timeless Truths, https://library.timelesstruths.org/music/I_Have_Decided_to_Follow_Jesus/. Accessed 23 March 2022.

vi. "Does the Song of Solomon Point to Jesus?" *BibleMesh.com*, Bible Mesh, https://biblemesh.com/blog/does-the-song-of-solomon-point-to-Jesus/. Accessed 12 June 2022.

vii. "Shulamite." *Name-Doctor.com*, Name Doctor, https://www.name-doctor.com/name-shulamite-meaning-of-shulamite-30142.html. Accessed 12 June 2022.

viii. "What Does Frankincense Symbolize in the Bible?" *ReligionAndCivilSociety.com*, Reliogion and Civil Society, https://religionandcivilsociety.com/bible/what-does-frankincense-symbolize-in-the-bible.html. Accessed 12 June 2022.

ix. "Meaning of White in the Bible." *BibleStudy.org*, Bible Study, https://www.biblestudy.org/bible-study-by-topic/meaning-of-colors-in-the-bible/meaning-of-color-white.html. Accessed 15 June 2022.

x. "Lisa." *SheKnows.com*, She Knows, https://www.sheknows.com/baby-names/name/lisa/. Accessed 15 June 2022.

xi. "Sandy." *SheKnows.com*, She Knows, https://www.sheknows.com/baby-names/name/sandy/. Accessed 25 June 2022.

xii. "The Number 2." *BibleStudy.org*, Bible Study, https://www.biblestudy.org/bibleref/meaning-of-numbers-in-bible/2.html. Accessed 25 June 2022.

xiii. "Covenant." *JewishJewels.org*, Jewish Jewels, https://www.jewishjewels.org/?s=covenant+sacred+of+all+binding+contracts. Accessed 25 June 2022.

xiv. "The Divine Colour Blue." *Blog.OUP.com*, OUPBlog, https://blog.oup.com/2014/10/divine-colour-blue-rublev-trinity/. Accessed 25 June 2022.

xv. "Insurance." *Lexico.com*, Lexico, https://www.lexico.com/en/definition/insurance. Accessed 25 June 2022.

xvi. "Best Answer: What does the name Theresa mean in the Bible? *ReligionAndCivilSociety.com*, Religion and Civil Society, https://religionandcivilsociety.com/bible/best-answer-what-does-the-name-theresa-mean-in-the-bible.html. Accessed 25 June 2022.

xvii. "David Baroni – A New Anointing for a New Day Lyrics." *TheLyricArchive.com*, The Lyric Archive, http://www.thelyricarchive.com/song/2789993-451272/A-New-Anointing-for-a-New-Day. Accessed 1 July 2022.

xviii. "Security Check." *CollinsDictionary.com*, Collins Dictionary, https://www.collinsdictionary.com/dictionary/english/security-check. Accessed 6 July 2022.

xix. "Receipt." *DreamBible.com*, Dream Bible, http://www.dream bible.com/search.php?q=Receipt. Accessed 6 July 2022.

xx. "Kairos." *Merriam-Webster.com*, Merriam-Webster Dictionary, https://www.merriam-webster.com/dictionary/kairos. Accessed 4 September 2022.

xxi. "Annie." *Kidadl.com*, Kidadl, https://kidadl.com/baby-names/meaning-of/annie. Accessed 14 September 2022.

xxii. "Annie." *SheKnows.com*, She Knows, https://www.sheknows.com/baby-names/name/annie/. Accessed 14 September 2022.

xxiii. "What do Horses Symbolize Spiritually in Dreams and the Bible?" *HorseRacingSense.com*, Horse Racing Sense, https://horseracingsense.com/what-do-horses-symbolize-art-dreams-bible/. Accessed 14 September 2022.

xxiv. "The Gates of Jerusalem in Nehemiah's Day." *IsraelMy Glory.org*, Israel My Glory, https://israelmyglory.org/article/the-gates-of-jerusalem-in-nehemiahs-day/. Accessed 14 September 2022.

xxv. "Meaning of Numbers in the Bible: The Number 8." *BibleStudy.org*, Bible Study, https://www.biblestudy.org/bibleref/meaning-of-numbers-in-bible/8.html. Accessed 14 September 2022.

xxvi. Shirk, John. "Q and A – What does it mean to kick against the goads?" *WJTL.com*, WJTL, https://wjtl.com/pages/q-and-a-what-does-it-mean-to-kick-against-the-goads/. Accessed 15 September 2022.

ACKNOWLEDGMENTS

Jessica Hallmark, what a joy you are to me! I can't express to you what a pleasure that it has been to work with you. God has given me the best editor and spiritual granddaughter in the world! Jesus has gifted you greatly, but I know that He has so much more for your life! There is an increase of glory coming into your life that will astound you!

Again, Holy Spirit, thank You for giving me the thoughts and inspiration to write this book. Every time I sat down to type, I felt Your glorious presence hovering over me and pouring into my soul Your words and Your desire for this book. Truly, You have been my "Helper" and my "Comforter," and I know that apart from You I can do nothing. What a joy it has been to "partner" with You!

ABOUT THE AUTHOR

Theresa Reyna lives in Cudahy, Wisconsin with her husband Ron. She has three grown children and eight grandchildren. She has a master's degree in Biblical studies and was ordained by Son Rise Ministries in November of 2009. Her earnest desire is to do the will of the Father and to accomplish her calling and destiny in Christ. Her passion is to see the Body of Christ riding the "High Wave of Glory" with Jesus in this *new era,* this *new day* of unprecedented miracles, signs, and wonders. Her desire is to see God's people *"all come to the unity of the faith and of the knowledge of the Son of God, to a perfect man, to the measure of the stature of the fullness of Christ"* (Ephesians 4:13b – NKJV.) This is Theresa's 6th book.

You can connect with her at www.lovecallsministry.com.